TIMED READINGS

Third Edition

Fifty 400-Word Passages
with Questions for
Building Reading Speed

BOOK EIGHT

Edward Spargo

JAMESTOWN PUBLISHERS

a division of NTC/CONTEMPORARY PUBLISHING GROUP
Lincolnwood, Illinois USA

Titles in This Series
Timed Readings, Third Edition
Timed Readings in Literature

Teaching Notes are available for this text and
will be sent to the instructor. Please write on
school stationery; tell us what grade
you teach and identify the text.

Timed Readings, Third Edition
Book Eight

Cover and text design: Deborah Hulsey Christie

ISBN: 0-89061-510-1

Published by Jamestown Publishers,
a division of NTC/Contemporary Publishing Group, Inc.,
4255 West Touhy Avenue,
Lincolnwood (Chicago), Illinois 60712-1975 U.S.A.
© 1989 by NTC/Contemporary Publishing Group, Inc.
Manufactured in the United States of America.
00 01 02 03 04 VH 14 13 12 11 10 9

Contents

Introduction to the Student

These *Timed Readings* are designed to help you become a faster and better reader. As you progress through the book, you will find yourself growing in reading speed and comprehension. You will be challenged to increase your reading rate while maintaining a high level of comprehension.

Reading, like most things, improves with practice. If you practice improving your reading speed, you will improve. As you will see, the rewards of improved reading speed will be well worth your time and effort.

Why Read Faster?

The quick and simple answer is that faster readers are better readers. Does this statement surprise you? You might think that fast readers would miss something and their comprehension might suffer. This is not true, for two reasons:

1. Faster readers comprehend faster. When you read faster, the writer's message is coming to you faster and makes sense sooner. Ideas are interconnected. The writer's thoughts are all tied together, each one leading to the next. The more quickly you can see how ideas are related to each other, the more quickly you can comprehend the meaning of what you are reading.

2. Faster readers concentrate better. Concentration is essential for comprehension. If your mind is wandering you can't understand what you are reading. A lack of concentration causes you to re-read, sometimes over and over, in order to comprehend. Faster readers concentrate better because there's less time for distractions to interfere. Comprehension, in turn, contributes to concentration. If you are concentrating and comprehending, you will not become distracted.

Want to Read More?

Do you wish that you could read more? (or, at least, would you like to do your required reading in less time?) Faster reading will help.

The illustration on the next page shows the number of books someone might read over a period of ten years. Let's see what faster reading could do for you. Look at the stack of books read by a slow reader and the stack

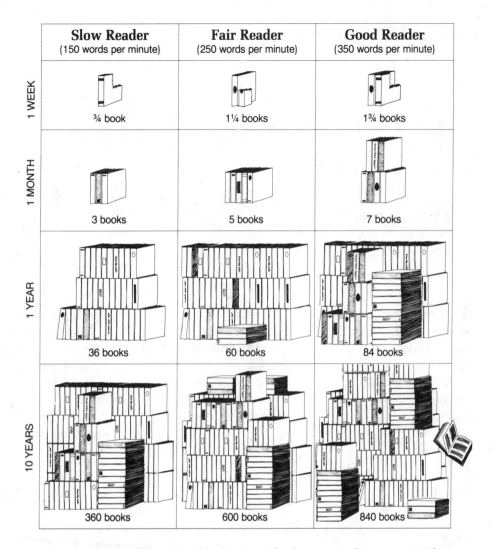

	Slow Reader (150 words per minute)	Fair Reader (250 words per minute)	Good Reader (350 words per minute)
1 WEEK	¾ book	1¼ books	1¾ books
1 MONTH	3 books	5 books	7 books
1 YEAR	36 books	60 books	84 books
10 YEARS	360 books	600 books	840 books

read by a good reader. (We show a speed of 350 words a minute for our "good" reader, but many fast readers can more than double that speed.) Let's say, however, that you are now reading at a rate of 150 words a minute. The illustration shows you reading 36 books a year. By increasing your reading speed to 250 words a minute, you could increase the number of books to 60 a year.

We have arrived at these numbers by assuming that the readers in our illustration read for one hour a day, six days a week, and that an average book is about 72,000 words long. Many people do not read that much, but they might if they could learn to read better and faster.

Faster reading doesn't *take* time, it *saves* time!

How to Use This Book

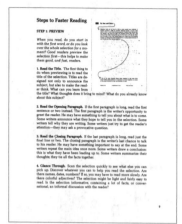

1 Learn the Four Steps Study and learn the four steps to follow to become a better and faster reader. The steps are covered on pages 9, 10, 11, and 12.

2 Preview Turn to the selection you are going to read and wait for the instructor's signal to preview. Your instructor will allow 30 seconds for previewing.

3 Begin reading When your instructor gives you the signal, begin reading. Read at a slightly faster-than-normal speed. Read well enough so that you will be able to answer questions about what you have read.

7 Fill in the progress graph Enter your score and plot your reading time on the graph on page 118 or 119. The right-hand side of the graph shows your words-per-minute reading speed. Write this number at the bottom of the page on the line labeled *Words per Minute.*

4 **Record your time**
When you finish reading, look at the blackboard and note your reading time. Your reading time will be the lowest time remaining on the board, or the next number to be erased. Write this time at the bottom of the page on the line labeled *Reading Time.*

5 **Answer the questions**
Answer the ten questions on the next page. There are five fact questions and five thought questions. Pick the *best* answer to each question and put an x in the box beside it.

6 **Correct your answers**
Using the Answer Key on pages 116 and 117, correct your work. Circle your wrong answers and put an x in the box you should have marked. Score 10 points for each correct answer. Write your score at the bottom of the page on the line labeled *Comprehension Score.*

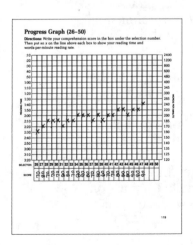

Instructions for the Pacing Drills

From time to time your instructor may wish to conduct pacing drills using *Timed Readings*. For this work you need to use the Pacing Dots printed in the margins of your book pages. The dots will help you regulate your reading speed to match the pace set by your instructor or announced on the reading cassette tape.

You will be reading at the correct pace if you are at the dot when your instructor says "Mark" or when you hear a tone on the tape. If you are ahead of the pace, read a little more slowly; if you are behind the pace, increase your reading speed. Try to match the pace exactly.

Follow these steps.

Step 1: Record the pace. At the bottom of the page, write on the line labeled *Words per Minute* the rate announced by the instructor or by the speaker on the tape.

Step 2: Begin reading. Wait for the signal to begin reading. Read at a slightly faster-than-normal speed. You will not know how on-target your pace is until you hear your instructor say "Mark" or until you hear the first tone on the tape. After a little practice you will be able to select an appropriate starting speed most of the time.

Step 3: Adjust your pace. As you read, try to match the pace set by the instructor or the tape. Read more slowly or more quickly as necessary. You should be reading the line beside the dot when you hear the pacing signal. The pacing sounds may distract you at first. Don't worry about it. Keep reading and your concentration will return.

Step 4: Stop and answer questions. Stop reading when you are told to, even if you have not finished the selection. Answer the questions right away. Correct your work and record your score on the line *Comprehension Score*. Strive to maintain 80 percent comprehension on each drill as you gradually increase your pace.

Step 5: Fill in the pacing graph. Transfer your words-per-minute rate to the box labeled *Pace* on the pacing graph on page 120. Then plot your comprehension score on the line above the box.

These pacing drills are designed to help you become a more flexible reader. They encourage you to "break out" of a pattern of reading everything at the same speed.

The drills help in other ways, too. Sometimes in a reading program you reach a certain level and bog down. You don't seem able to move on and progress. The pacing drills will help you to work your way out of such slumps and get your reading program moving again.

Steps to Faster Reading

STEP 1: PREVIEW

When you read, do you start in with the first word, or do you look over the whole selection for a moment? Good readers preview the selection first—this helps to make them good, and fast, readers.

1. Read the Title. The first thing to do when previewing is to read the title of the selection. Titles are designed not only to announce the subject, but also to make the reader think. What can you learn from the title? What thoughts does it bring to mind? What do you already know about this subject?

2. Read the Opening Paragraph. If the first paragraph is long, read the first sentence or two instead. The first paragraph is the writer's opportunity to greet the reader. He may have something to tell you about what is to come. Some writers announce what they hope to tell you in the selection. Some writers tell why they are writing. Some writers just try to get the reader's attention—they may ask a provocative question.

3. Read the Closing Paragraph. If the last paragraph is long, read just the final line or two. The closing paragraph is the writer's last chance to talk to his reader. He may have something important to say at the end. Some writers repeat the main idea once more. Some writers draw a conclusion: this is what they have been leading up to. Some writers summarize their thoughts; they tie all the facts together.

4. Glance Through. Scan the selection quickly to see what else you can pick up. Discover whatever you can to help you read the selection. Are there names, dates, numbers? If so, you may have to read more slowly. Are there colorful adjectives? The selection might be light and fairly easy to read. Is the selection informative, containing a lot of facts, or conversational, an informal discussion with the reader?

flying towers normal stage migration. some cruising pelicans, time subtle scientists close

Steps to Faster Reading

STEP 2: READ FOR MEANING

When you read, do you just see words? Are you so occupied reading words that you sometimes fail to get the meaning? Good readers see beyond the words—they read for meaning. This makes them faster readers.

1. Build Concentration. You cannot read with understanding if you are not concentrating. Every reader's mind wanders occasionally; it is not a cause for alarm. When you discover that your thoughts have strayed, correct the situation right away. The longer you wait, the harder it becomes. Avoid distractions and distracting situations. Outside noises and activities will compete for your attention if you let them. Keep the preview information in mind as you read. This will help to focus your attention on the selection.

2. Read in Thought Groups. Individual words do not tell us much. They must be combined with other words in order to yield meaning. To obtain meaning from the printed page, therefore, the reader should see the words in meaningful combinations. If you see only a word at a time (called word-by-word reading), your comprehension suffers along with your speed. To improve both speed and comprehension, try to group the words into phrases which have a natural relationship to each other. For practice, you might want to read aloud, trying to speak the words in meaningful combinations.

3. Question the Author. To sustain the pace you have set for yourself, and to maintain a high level of comprehension, question the writer as you read. Continually ask yourself such questions as, "What does this mean? What is he saying now? How can I use this information?" Questions like these help you to concentrate fully on the selection.

Steps to Faster Reading

STEP 3: GRASP
PARAGRAPH SENSE

The paragraph is the basic unit of meaning. If you can discover quickly and understand the main point of each paragraph, you can comprehend the author's message. Good readers know how to find the main ideas of paragraphs quickly. This helps to make them faster readers.

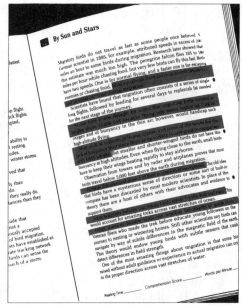

1. Find the Topic Sentence. The topic sentence, the sentence containing the main idea, is often the first sentence of a paragraph. It is followed by other sentences which support, develop, or explain the main idea. Sometimes a topic sentence comes at the end of a paragraph. When it does, the supporting details come first, building the base for the topic sentence. Some paragraphs do not have a topic sentence. Such paragraphs usually create a mood or feeling, rather than present information.

2. Understand Paragraph Structure. Every well-written paragraph has purpose. The purpose may be to inform, define, explain, persuade, compare or contrast, illustrate, and so on. The purpose should always relate to the main idea and expand on it. As you read each paragraph, see how the body of the paragraph is used to tell you more about the main idea or topic sentence. Read the supporting details intelligently, recognizing that what you are reading is all designed to develop the single main idea.

Steps to Faster Reading

STEP 4: ORGANIZE FACTS

When you read, do you tend to see a lot of facts without any apparent connection or relationship? Understanding how the facts all fit together to deliver the author's message is, after all, the reason for reading. Good readers organize facts as they read. This helps them to read rapidly and well.

1. Discover the Writer's Plan. Look for a clue or signal word early in the article which might reveal the author's structure. Every writer has a plan or outline which he follows. If the reader can discover his method of organization, he has the key to understanding the message. Sometimes the author gives you obvious signals. If he says, "There are three reasons . . ." the wise reader looks for a listing of the three items. Other less obvious signal words such as *moreover, otherwise, consequently* all tell the reader the direction the writer's message will take.

2. Relate as You Read. As you read the selection, keep the information learned during the preview in mind. See how the ideas you are reading all fit into place. Consciously strive to relate what you are reading to the title. See how the author is carrying through in his attempt to piece together a meaningful message. As you discover the relationship among the ideas, the message comes through quickly and clearly.

Timed
Reading
Selections

1   Clues to the Past

Archaeology is the recovery and interpretation of objects and information that together provide clues to the past. These clues often are thought of as coming solely from the objects that have remained from the culture of past peoples.

The purpose of archaeology is to get a first-hand glimpse, through the clues available, of what it was like to live in past times. The challenge is to learn to discover evidence without destroying it. This takes knowledge of how to recover evidence carefully, what to observe, and what to do with what is found. Also, one must know what objects and records above ground are of value and how to record and preserve them.

The precise location of everything that is found, together with identification of soils, structures, and all other associations is often of crucial importance in our efforts to interpret and understand what has happened in the past.

Archaeology is not limited to the buried past or remote ages. It is a technique for discovering and conserving evidence of all times and places. It extends its inquiry both below and above ground.

Because most schools do not have faculty members who are trained archaeologists, or historians who do research, or museum conservationists who preserve objects or data of historical value, this program is largely up to the individual student to implement on her own, with what help she can find among trained professionals in the community. But there are many teachers who are trained and enthusiastic conservators and researchers, and their help can be of great value.

An important part of archaeological conservation is knowing what kind of site is best protected by the earth that covers it. Invariably, sites are better left untouched than excavated by unskilled hands.

Archaeology requires many patiently-acquired skills. Below ground archaeology must be attempted only by trained and skilled people who work carefully and scientifically. Archaeology should never be done simply for fun or simply to collect objects. Training for field archaeology, laboratory procedure, and report writing can be acquired only by working closely with a trained and qualified archaeologist, either a professional or nonprofessional. It is absolutely essential that one have this instruction and be led by trained archaeologists before attempting to investigate an archaeological site, prehistoric or historic. Archaeology is no do-it-yourself hobby for the uninstructed. Many archaeologists spend years researching an area before even attempting to dig at an archaeological site.

Recalling Facts

1. According to the author, archaeology should not be attempted simply for
   - ☐ a. fun.
   - ☐ b. learning.
   - ☐ c. research.

2. The archaeologist who is working in the field must record
   - ☐ a. the time of day.
   - ☐ b. the exact location.
   - ☐ c. the tools used.

3. The author feels that nonprofessional archaeologists are
   - ☐ a. unqualified to dig.
   - ☐ b. unskilled.
   - ☐ c. often well trained.

4. An archaeologist can be expected to
   - ☐ a. write reports.
   - ☐ b. work without pay.
   - ☐ c. work alone.

5. An archaeologist must be an expert in recognizing
   - ☐ a. coins.
   - ☐ b. pottery.
   - ☐ c. soils.

Understanding the Passage

6. Archaeologists must be careful about
   - ☐ a. preserving evidence.
   - ☐ b. trespassing on private property.
   - ☐ c. digging on historic locations.

7. The author's purpose is to
   - ☐ a. define archaeology.
   - ☐ b. explain age-old customs.
   - ☐ c. discuss excavation sites in the Old World.

8. This article is directed to
   - ☐ a. archaeologists who are seeking information about their work.
   - ☐ b. people who are interested in archaeology.
   - ☐ c. school teachers who wish to teach archaeology.

9. The author stresses the archaeologist's need for
   - ☐ a. skill.
   - ☐ b. punctuality.
   - ☐ c. determination.

10. We can conclude that archaeology
    - ☐ a. is a good do-it-yourself hobby.
    - ☐ b. is not considered an important subject.
    - ☐ c. research can result in interesting historical reports.

2   Those Daring Young Men

Exhibition flight, one of the most glamorous phases of aviation, started with the very beginning of flight. Flying for entertainment, thrills, prizes, or for sheer joy is a different dimension of flight than general aviation, military flying, or test flying.

Much early exhibition flight was connected with ballooning. The first free balloon ascension of the Montgolfier brothers in Paris was an exhibition flight. The history of ballooning and dirigible flight is filled with exhibition flights, including carnival shows, racing, and record attempts.

Early in 1910 the Wright brothers formed an exhibition team that made its debut in Indianapolis. Two of the most famous pilots on this team were Arch Hoxsey and Ralph Johnstone, The Heavenly Twins. Their daring aerobatic duels thrilled spectators until they were killed within a month of each other late in 1910. Glenn Curtiss also formed an exhibition team, which included Eugene Ely and Beckwith Havens, as well as the legendary Lincoln Beachey. The rivalry between the two teams generated interest throughout the country.

Lincoln Beachey, who had been a dirigible pilot, became the most famous exhibition flyer of those early years. After training with the Curtiss team, he made his first exhibition tour in early 1911. He soon developed the techniques that were to make him famous. His complete lack of fear, coupled with his great flying skill and showman's talents, allowed him to do things in an airplane that had hitherto been believed impossible. He was the first American to do a loop and the first to fly upside down. He often flew in front of the crowd at minimum altitude with both hands off the controls. He usually concluded his act by performing his death dip, diving vertically from about 5,000 feet, pulling out at the last possible second, and landing right in front of the grandstand.

On one occasion, he flew over Niagara Falls, down into the gorge, and under the bridge. He also raced his airplane against cars driven by Barney Oldfield and Eddie Rickenbacker. In one year Beachey performed 1,000 loops before 17 million people in 126 cities. Beachey was killed in 1915 when the wings fell from his new monoplane while he was performing a vertical-S over San Francisco Bay.

World War I greatly advanced airplane development. During the war, both sides discovered the value of the airplane for locating enemy forces and military bases. The airplane's speed ability increased significantly.

Recalling Facts

1. One of the earliest airplane exhibition flights occurred in
   - ☐ a. 1895.
   - ☐ b. 1910.
   - ☐ c. 1921.

2. Arch Hoxsey and Ralph Johnstone were billed as
   - ☐ a. The Heavenly Twins.
   - ☐ b. The Fearless Duo.
   - ☐ c. The Balloon Brothers.

3. The first American to fly upside down was
   - ☐ a. Wilbur Wright.
   - ☐ b. Eugene Ely.
   - ☐ c. Lincoln Beachey.

4. The author does not mention a
   - ☐ a. monoplane.
   - ☐ b. dirigible.
   - ☐ c. glider.

5. Lincoln Beachey was killed when the plane lost its
   - ☐ a. engine.
   - ☐ b. wings.
   - ☐ c. controls.

Understanding the Passage

6. In this selection Eddie Rickenbacker is associated with
   - ☐ a. stunt flights.
   - ☐ b. balloon ascents.
   - ☐ c. auto races.

7. The article suggests that
   - ☐ a. nature is more powerful than man.
   - ☐ b. people enjoy carnivals and fairs.
   - ☐ c. man finds sport in meeting danger.

8. The author implies that
   - ☐ a. exhibition flying is more dangerous than test flying.
   - ☐ b. women are not usually part of stunt teams.
   - ☐ c. balloon flights preceded plane exhibitions.

9. The death dip involved
   - ☐ a. flying upside down under a bridge.
   - ☐ b. plunging thousands of feet to a safe landing.
   - ☐ c. landing with retracted wheels.

10. We can conclude that
   - ☐ a. exhibition flying had its beginnings in France.
   - ☐ b. no one has been able to duplicate the stunts of Beachey.
   - ☐ c. the Wright brothers did all of their flying in Virginia.

3   Leukemia Therapy

Research in leukemia therapy has kept pace with studies of causes of the disease and has shown a greater measure of success. In the 1950s, a leukemic child lived only three months after diagnosis. Today, most youngsters live five years or longer after diagnosis. And an increasing number treated with anticancer drugs appear completely cured of the disease.

The remarkable increases in survival are due to very effective use of chemotherapy, radiation therapy, blood transfusion, and improved auxiliary therapy for complications. Many of these procedures were developed through studies conducted at leukemia research centers throughout the United States. For example, St. Jude Children's Research Hospital in Memphis has been conducting a series of total therapy studies which has resulted in three-year continuous remissions, or disappearance of all signs of disease, among 61 percent of a group of children with acute lymphocytic leukemia. In addition to receiving multiple-agent chemotherapy, these young patients were given central nervous system irradiation early in remission.

A remission is a temporary stop of the leukemic process. When a remission occurs, there is often a complete return to the normal state. The symptoms disappear, the physical findings become normal, and the abnormal cells are no longer found in the bone marrow. Sometimes the remission is only partial, and one or more of the signs of leukemia may not completely disappear. Unfortunately, most remissions are only temporary and there are patients who never have one. Tests of the blood at frequent intervals and of the bone marrow enable the leukemia specialists to follow the course of the disease and to select the proper dosage of the appropriate drug.

Leukemia therapy had its beginning in November 1947, when Dr. Sidney Farber and his colleagues at the children's Cancer Research Foundation, Boston, pioneered the use of aminopterin. They induced temporary remissions in ten children with acute leukemia. These remissions were the first to be achieved by any form of therapy.

Scientists have found that the interaction of two or more drugs produces a combination with greater ability to induce remissions than any one individual drug. Combinations of these drugs can be used because the harmful effects of each drug are different. In combination, each drug can be used at full dose, that is, the dose used when each is used alone. Intensive treatment with combinations of drugs active against the acute leukemias is the most important recent advance in leukemia research.

Recalling Facts

1. A leukemic child lived only three months after diagnosis during the
   - ☐ a. 1940s.
   - ☐ b. 1950s.
   - ☐ c. 1960s.

2. Today, most children with leukemia
   - ☐ a. are undiagnosed.
   - ☐ b. live less than three years.
   - ☐ c. live more than five years.

3. Remissions are usually
   - ☐ a. shocking.
   - ☐ b. unnoticeable.
   - ☐ c. temporary.

4. Leukemia therapy had its beginnings in
   - ☐ a. 1939.
   - ☐ b. 1947.
   - ☐ c. 1957.

5. When used in combination, each drug is given at
   - ☐ a. half-strength.
   - ☐ b. full dose.
   - ☐ c. different times.

Understanding the Passage

6. The St. Jude Children's Hospital has shown success in treating leukemia of the
   - ☐ a. lymph glands.
   - ☐ b. blood cells.
   - ☐ c. pancreas.

7. When a complete remission occurs, the patient
   - ☐ a. seems to be taking a turn for the worse.
   - ☐ b. appears to be cured of the disease.
   - ☐ c. begins to reject medications.

8. The author states that
   - ☐ a. vitamins are beginning to play a major role in leukemia cures.
   - ☐ b. leukemia research has been funded by the federal government.
   - ☐ c. drug dosages are made according to blood examinations.

9. According to the article, leukemia sometimes
   - ☐ a. paralyzes the arms and legs.
   - ☐ b. goes away by itself without treatment.
   - ☐ c. does not respond to chemotherapy.

10. We can conclude that
   - ☐ a. the cause of leukemia can be traced to genetic imbalances.
   - ☐ b. fatigue and weakness are the first signs of leukemia.
   - ☐ c. many hospitals are experimenting with leukemia drugs.

4 Following the Rules

The United States Environmental Protection Agency (EPA) was established to lead the nation's fight against pollution. It reports directly to the President.

It is in charge of federal programs to control air and water pollution and other environmental problems caused by solid wastes, pesticides, radiation, and noise. Its authority to control pollution by setting standards and enforcing regulations is made possible by the laws passed by Congress.

The President, with the consent of Congress, decided it was best to have a single, independent agency so that all environmental problems could be considered as a whole. In this way, we can be sure that in reducing air pollution, for example, we don't add to water pollution or make some other environmental problem worse.

All levels of government and all citizens must join the effort to save our environment. To help them, EPA has set up ten regional offices in different parts of the country. EPA's regional specialists are experts in pollution prevention and control. They also know a lot about the problems of their area.

EPA stops people from polluting by setting and enforcing environmental standards. These standards define the kinds and amounts of pollutants that must be kept from entering our environment.

The standards also set up timetables for cleaning up pollution. Sometimes everyone must stop putting a particular chemical into air or water or on crops and fields. This is done if the pollutant is dangerous. If there is no immediate danger, some time may be allowed to install machinery in manufacturing plants or make other changes to remove the pollutant.

For some types of pollution, EPA has the authority to set standards and enforce them. For others, most authority is with the state or local governments. The authority depends on the nature of the problem. In general, Congress decided that strong federal authority is needed to curb pollution that crosses state boundaries, or where it would be difficult for the states to enforce the laws, such as in making sure all new cars are low-polluting. Problems, like keeping streets clean or collecting garbage or building parks, are handled by state and local governments.

EPA is concerned with the big problems of national pollution and makes sure that the same rules are followed all over the country. It uses the best research and knowledge available to decide what is harmful in the environment and what should be banned or limited.

Recalling Facts

1. EPA reports directly to the
   - ☐ a. Department of the Interior.
   - ☐ b. Secretary of State.
   - ☐ c. President.

2. EPA is not directly concerned with
   - ☐ a. radiation.
   - ☐ b. noise.
   - ☐ c. recreation.

3. How many regional offices does EPA operate?
   - ☐ a. five
   - ☐ b. ten
   - ☐ c. fifteen

4. The task of building new parks is handled by
   - ☐ a. civic groups.
   - ☐ b. local governments.
   - ☐ c. the Department of State.

5. EPA's authority to control pollution was granted by the
   - ☐ a. Vice President.
   - ☐ b. United Nations.
   - ☐ c. Congress.

Understanding the Passage

6. The author implies that EPA is
   - ☐ a. restricting the use of pesticides.
   - ☐ b. advising industries to use coal for fuel.
   - ☐ c. warning people not to use detergents.

7. According to the article,
   - ☐ a. pollution is a problem everywhere in the world.
   - ☐ b. carbon monoxide is the most deadly gas known.
   - ☐ c. some pollutants are more dangerous than others.

8. Some industries are allowed to
   - ☐ a. set aside tracts of land for sewage disposal.
   - ☐ b. remove pollutants by mechanical means.
   - ☐ c. dump wastes in nearby rivers and streams.

9. EPA was established to control
   - ☐ a. pollution in low-income areas.
   - ☐ b. interstate pollution.
   - ☐ c. urban pollution only.

10. We can conclude that
    - ☐ a. the work of EPA covers all phases of pollution.
    - ☐ b. EPA is still in the planning stages.
    - ☐ c. many people resent the work of EPA.

Three Masters

Starting with George Washington and ending with Washington, D.C., the Potomac in its time has served three masters. The first two of the significant "users" were also famous abusers of the river. Likewise, the Washington metropolitan region, which is today the prime user of the Potomac, is also its greatest polluter. In the history of the Potomac, it appears that major abuses are inevitably linked to major uses.

The Potomac in George Washington's day was the only river of great economic importance. The aristocratic Tidewater society, which the first President represented, was one largely engaged in raising crops—mainly tobacco—for export to the Old World. Since little was known and less was done about land erosion by Washington and his fellow plantation owners, much of their soil was lost to the river. The loss of soil proved to be the loss of the lifeblood of this early society. The resulting sediment destroyed fish life and hampered navigation.

Opportunity subsequently moved upstream. During the next century the Potomac served the mining industry, rather than agriculture. Coal was discovered in George's Creek in 1808. Washington's dream of a navigational link with the West was sought through the building of the Chesapeake and Ohio Canal extending from Washington to Cumberland, Maryland. During the years of 1907 and 1908, the most productive mine in the world operated in the George's Creek Valley—the No. 7 Mine of the Consolidation Coal Company, with an average output of 5,700 tons per day. Like Tidewater agriculture, the underground exploitation upstream lasted for about 100 years.

Coal mining waned about 1910 with a temporary revival during World War I, leaving a heritage of pollution. The heritage was not sediment as in Tidewater but the destructive acid mine drainage which still inhibits the use of the North Branch waters. The Chesapeake and Ohio Canal could not counter the competition of the growing railroad industry, and barge traffic was halted in 1924.

In post-World War II times, major economic opportunity lay once again on the estuary at Washington, D.C. The area is now highly populated and thriving. Today the Potomac is primarily in the service of this important "World Capital." Agriculture is now lodged upstream, while the river's limited number of industries reside principally along the North Branch and along the Shenandoah. Washington, D.C., where the principal economic opportunities lie, is by far the single greatest user of water in the basin.

Recalling Facts

1. The Tidewater society was mostly involved with
   □ a. restoring buildings.
   □ b. raising money.
   □ c. planting crops.

2. Washington was not concerned with the problems of
   □ a. federal spending.
   □ b. import quotas.
   □ c. soil erosion.

3. The Chesapeake and Ohio Canal extends from Washington, D.C., into
   □ a. Delaware.
   □ b. Maryland.
   □ c. West Virginia.

4. The No. 7 Mine of the Consolidation Coal Company once produced
   □ a. nearly 1,000 tons of coal per day.
   □ b. more than 5,000 tons of coal per day.
   □ c. approximately 10,000 tons of coal per day.

5. Barge traffic was halted on the Potomac River during the middle
   □ a. 1920s.
   □ b. 1930s.
   □ c. 1940s.

Understanding the Passage

6. The Potomac was first used in conjunction with
   □ a. agriculture.
   □ b. industry.
   □ c. mining.

7. The title of this article refers to three
   □ a. areas of human activity on the Potomac.
   □ b. Presidents who tried to end pollution in the Potomac.
   □ c. civic groups that aroused interest in water pollution.

8. Barge traffic on the Chesapeake and Ohio Canal ended because
   □ a. the Canal was becoming too polluted.
   □ b. mining companies bought the land on both sides of the Canal.
   □ c. the railroad charged lower rates.

9. The Tidewater society was comprised of
   □ a. veterans of the Revolutionary War.
   □ b. wealthy and influential people.
   □ c. residents of Jamestown, Virginia.

10. Tobacco could not be grown along the Potomac after a while because
    □ a. England refused to buy products from the colonies.
    □ b. the Potomac changed its course and isolated fertile lands.
    □ c. erosion washed much productive soil into the Potomac.

6 Liquids, Granules, and Powders

Scientists tell us that there are from three to ten million known species of insects in the world. Thousands more are identified every year. Many of the known insects feed on living plants. Some, such as butterflies and moths in the larval stage, can seriously damage a whole field or forest. Yet later, as adults, they carry the pollen that insures the growth of new plants. Some insects are harmful to man because they are disease carriers. Some are just unpleasant nuisances. Many others are beneficial because they destroy insects that cause damage.

In the United States, we have been using various chemicals for many years to control insect pests. Among the earliest insecticides were sulfurs and compounds containing arsenic. Light oils were often used to control mosquitoes. Later, man-made organic compounds were developed. Some of these kill insects long after they are applied. Chemicals called herbicides were developed to control undesirable plant growth; others known as fungicides protected plants from diseases. Chemicals are also used to control pests, such as rodents. By now, thousands of such pesticides in liquid, granule, and powder form have been used in the United States.

We know, of course, that these chemicals can be good. They have enabled us to increase food production, and they have controlled such killing diseases as malaria and encephalitis. We know now, however, that some of these compounds may also seriously damage our environment.

Some of the newer pesticides are called persistent compounds because they do not break down readily in nature's recycling system. This is especially true of chlorinated hydrocarbons such as DDT. They persist in the environment and eventually accumulate in the tissues of birds, fish, wildlife, and even man. As larger species feed on smaller ones, more and more chemicals are concentrated in their tissues. Some predatory birds, fish, and animals may accumulate levels several thousand times the concentration found in the water, air, or plants around them because they receive all the chemicals stored by all the animals in their food chain.

Man is at the top of this food chain. The average American now carries about eight parts per million of DDT in his fatty tissues. We do not know if this amount is harmful to humans. However, we have known for some years that DDT kills fish, and there is evidence that it threatens other desirable wildlife species. The consequences of DDT will probably be realized in the future.

Recalling Facts

1. Some scientists think that the total number of insect species is
   - ☐ a. two million.
   - ☐ b. ten million.
   - ☐ c. sixteen million.

2. One of the earliest insecticides was
   - ☐ a. glycerine.
   - ☐ b. cyanide.
   - ☐ c. sulfur.

3. Mosquitoes were often controlled with
   - ☐ a. oil.
   - ☐ b. potassium.
   - ☐ c. acid.

4. Chemicals have helped scientists to control
   - ☐ a. polio.
   - ☐ b. scarlet fever.
   - ☐ c. malaria.

5. A chemical that controls undesirable plant growth is called
   - ☐ a. a pesticide.
   - ☐ b. an herbicide.
   - ☐ c. a fungicide.

Understanding the Passage

6. According to the author, persistent compounds
   - ☐ a. work effectively to kill rodents for many months.
   - ☐ b. can cause brain damage in young animals.
   - ☐ c. do not break down in a natural recycling system.

7. DDT is dangerous because it
   - ☐ a. is carried high into the atmosphere.
   - ☐ b. is not soluble in water.
   - ☐ c. accumulates in the tissues of all living things.

8. The author is concerned about
   - ☐ a. human consumption of products containing pesticides.
   - ☐ b. the widespread use of organic fertilizers.
   - ☐ c. indiscriminate use of herbicides.

9. The author of this article might be
   - ☐ a. a newspaper reporter.
   - ☐ b. a chemical manufacturer.
   - ☐ c. an ecologist.

10. We can conclude that chemicals
    - ☐ a. cannot be used in vegetable gardens.
    - ☐ b. are known to be completely safe.
    - ☐ c. may cause great harm to living creatures.

7　A Unique Reporting System

Land prices are by no means a concern only of farmers. Many important decisions in the business world involve some aspect of land valuation. For instance, a major communications firm wants to build relay stations across the country and needs estimates of land costs. For space exploration projects, a spot on earth is needed to launch satellites and to receive their messages. A life insurance company in Hartford, Connecticut, needs to know the level and trend in farmland prices and the income farmers are likely to earn to repay their loans.

A writer for a national business magazine wants to compare returns from owning farmland with returns from stocks and other investments. The administrator of a federal or state agency is budgeting the probable costs of acquiring rights-of-way for a highway, or land for an airport or a sewage disposal plant.

Letters and phone calls posing such questions flow to an office of the Economic Research Service in Washington, D.C. Here, research economists have access to a large volume of statistical data on farmland values for most areas of the country. And they are constantly adding to their stockpile of information with the aid of a nationwide corps of special reporters.

This reporting system has some rather interesting features. One group of reporters consists of the regular crop reporters—mostly farmers—who provide a regular flow of crop and livestock information to state offices of the Statistical Reporting Service. This agency, assisted by a large staff of volunteer reporters, serves farmers and consumers by issuing regular reports on a wide range of farm subjects. Crop conditions, acreages, yields, livestock numbers, and prices are covered in these reports.

Twice a year these reporters, who represent the eyes and ears of the U.S. Department of Agriculture, send in their estimates of the going market values of farm real estate in their areas. State statisticians review these reports and send on to Washington summaries for each reporting district. These are the data used to measure changes in market values state by state.

These figures are used chiefly to measure the relationship between prices at different points in time. Because the area is quite large, they can't be applied to an individual farm. Selling prices can vary greatly within a township or a county. It takes a detailed appraisal to determine what any particular tract of land is most likely to sell for.

Recalling Facts

1. The author mentions an insurance company located in
   □ a. Vermont.
   □ b. New Jersey.
   □ c. Connecticut.

2. The Economic Research Service consists of economists and
   □ a. special reporters.
   □ b. wholesalers.
   □ c. senators.

3. The Economic Research Service is associated with the Department of
   □ a. State.
   □ b. Commerce.
   □ c. Agriculture.

4. The Economic Research Service reports on
   □ a. climate trends.
   □ b. livestock numbers.
   □ c. export quotas.

5. Most of the reporters working for the Statistical Reporting Service are
   □ a. unpaid volunteers.
   □ b. paid after they make their reports.
   □ c. paid monthly out of state funds.

Understanding the Passage

6. We can assume that the Economic Research Service
   □ a. works closely with the President.
   □ b. answers questions submitted by the public.
   □ c. carries out most of its work in college libraries.

7. This article is concerned mostly with
   □ a. land values.
   □ b. inflation.
   □ c. property taxes.

8. According to the author, the selling price of land
   □ a. is uniform throughout the country.
   □ b. varies widely within a county.
   □ c. is affected regionally by minimum wages.

9. The Economic Research Service updates its information
   □ a. every week.
   □ b. every other month.
   □ c. twice a year.

10. The article suggests that
    □ a. land is often purchased as an investment.
    □ b. property taxes have increased steadily during the past ten years.
    □ c. the most expensive farmland is located in the Midwest.

8   The Hearts of His Countrymen

George Washington's death cast the entire nation into mourning. And when the sad news reached Europe, that continent, too, lamented. The London *Morning Chronicle* declared, "The long life of General Washington is not stained by a single blot ... His fame, bounded by no country, will be confined to no age." Napoleon ordered a ten-day requiem throughout France. Dirges were played in Amsterdam. In America, President John Adams ordered the Army to wear crepe armbands for six months, and in cities and towns, ladies donned black as though they were mourning for a member of the family. At Philadelphia, the Congress adjourned immediately and set December 26 as a day for formal mourning. That day, from the pulpit of the Lutheran Church, Virginia Congressman Henry Lee, who had known Washington so well and so long, spoke publicly the words that have never been forgotten: "First in war, first in peace, and first in the hearts of his countrymen."

A grieving and admiring Congress immediately resolved to erect a marble monument in the capital city. The House passed a $200,000 appropriation, but the Senate considered the measure for one year, then let it die. For the next 33 years, except for an occasional fruitless expression of interest in the halls of Congress, the project languished.

Then in 1833, influential citizens of Washington, led by George Watterson, who had been the first librarian of Congress, organized the Washington National Monument Society to raise by private subscription the memorial that Congress had forgotten. From designs submitted in competition, the work of Robert Mills, an eminent architect, was selected. It pictured a grand circular colonnaded building, 259 feet in diameter and 100 feet high, from whose top rose a decorated Egyptian obelisk 500 feet high. Its total height of 600 feet would make it the highest spire in the world.

Dollar donations were solicited from the public, but response was disappointingly slow. It was not until 1847 that $87,000, a sum sufficient for a beginning, was raised. President James K. Polk, with the assent of Congress, selected the site on public lands, upwards of 30 acres, "so elevated that the Monument will be seen from all parts of the city," as indeed it is today. On the sunny Fourth of July, 1848, Benjamin B. French, Grand Master of the District of Columbia Masonic Lodge, laid the cornerstone of the monument.

Recalling Facts

1. When Washington died, Napoleon ordered a requiem lasting
   - ☐ a. 10 days.
   - ☐ b. 20 days.
   - ☐ c. 30 days.

2. At the time of Washington's death, the President was
   - ☐ a. Adams.
   - ☐ b. Jefferson.
   - ☐ c. Madison.

3. The Congress set aside a day of mourning in
   - ☐ a. December.
   - ☐ b. March.
   - ☐ c. July.

4. The height of the Washington Monument is
   - ☐ a. 200 feet.
   - ☐ b. 400 feet.
   - ☐ c. 600 feet.

5. The cornerstone of the Washington Monument was laid during the
   - ☐ a. early 1800s.
   - ☐ b. middle 1800s.
   - ☐ c. late 1800s.

Understanding the Passage

6. The design for the Washington Monument was
   - ☐ a. inspired by the Paris City Hall.
   - ☐ b. the result of competitive submissions.
   - ☐ c. a composite design made from several drawings.

7. The Washington Monument was financed by
   - ☐ a. contributions from large corporations.
   - ☐ b. funds from the government.
   - ☐ c. donations from individuals.

8. The building of the Washington Monument was delayed for many years because
   - ☐ a. land could not be found for the memorial.
   - ☐ b. the House of Representatives would not consider the issue.
   - ☐ c. support for the idea was slow to develop.

9. The British press considered Washington to be
   - ☐ a. an outstanding world figure.
   - ☐ b. a simple and humble man.
   - ☐ c. America's finest President.

10. This article is primarily about the
   - ☐ a. presidency of Washington.
   - ☐ b. death of Washington.
   - ☐ c. building of an appropriate memorial.

Cones and Domes

Spacecraft photography has verified the fact that craters outnumber any other type of feature on the moon. Today, scientists generally believe that most of the craters were formed as a result of attack by cosmic debris. But volcanic activity has also played an important part in forming many craters and in determining the nature of the moon's surface.

Many impact craters can be classified as either primary or secondary. Primary craters are formed by the impact of cosmic debris that reaches the moon from outer space. Secondary craters are formed by the impact of blocky material that was thrown out during the primary event. Large primary craters are commonly flat-floored and many display central peaks. Small primary craters and the secondary craters commonly have rounded cup-shaped floors.

Craters range in size from small pits to the giants that measure hundreds of miles in diameter. Small craters are vastly more abundant than large ones. A tally of craters in various size categories provides a rough measure of the rates of bombardment. Micrometeoroids often bombard the moon. Large meteorites strike less frequently and, perhaps once in hundreds of thousands of years, a comet or asteroid collides with the moon to form a giant crater.

Some of the large craters on the moon resemble certain volcanic features called calderas on earth. They are formed by the collapse of surface rock into the underlying magma chamber from which molten material was removed at the time of an eruption. Other features on the moon resemble those that characterize volcanic fields on the earth, such as domes, cones, and surface flows. Some of these craters are found on the tops of small mountains.

The possibility that volcanic activity takes place on the moon is supported by many reports of the observation of red spots, white spots, and other transient phenomena. Infrared photographs show variations in surface temperature across the moon. Even though differential absorption of sunlight may account for some of this variation, part of it may be the result of heat transmitted from below the surface.

Some craters on the moon, perhaps formed by impacts, are partly flooded by volcanic materials. Fractures in the floors of these craters may have served as vents from which molten material flowed. In some places this material can be seen as "ponds," settling only in lower levels. In others, the flooding continued until the entire crater floor was covered.

Recalling Facts

1. Most moon craters were formed as a result of
   ☐ a. evolution.
   ☐ b. volcanic activity.
   ☐ c. cosmic bombardment.

2. Large primary craters have
   ☐ a. flat floors.
   ☐ b. concave floors.
   ☐ c. jagged floors.

3. Large meteors strike the moon on an average of once every
   ☐ a. 100 years.
   ☐ b. 6,000 years.
   ☐ c. 200,000 years.

4. According to the article, calderas are
   ☐ a. meteorites.
   ☐ b. rock minerals.
   ☐ c. volcanic formations.

5. Red and white spots on the moon's surface may indicate
   ☐ a. volcanic activity.
   ☐ b. water vapor.
   ☐ c. small craters.

Understanding the Passage

6. The author implies that
   ☐ a. meteors that do not hit the moon often strike the earth.
   ☐ b. craters are still being formed on the moon's surface.
   ☐ c. water evaporates rapidly on the moon.

7. Volcanoes on the moon
   ☐ a. often form inside craters.
   ☐ b. are usually restricted to the highest mountains.
   ☐ c. cause dense smoke on the dark side.

8. From the information provided, the reader can assume that
   ☐ a. domes are larger than cones.
   ☐ b. asteroids are larger than meteorites.
   ☐ c. white spots are larger than red spots.

9. A magma chamber is formed by
   ☐ a. a collapse of surface rocks.
   ☐ b. erosion of underlying minerals.
   ☐ c. an eruption of molten materials.

10. Infrared photographs are able to detect
    ☐ a. differences in surface temperature.
    ☐ b. pockets of water vapor.
    ☐ c. refraction and reflection of light.

10 The Blues

When a person feels low, blue, or down in the dumps, it usually means he's been hurt, disappointed, or saddened by something that causes a confused and listless feeling. There is even a type of music called "the blues," a low, mournful, wailing sound to express these universal human feelings.

Depression is another name for this mood. Feeling depressed is a normal and natural response to experiences of loss, failure, and bad luck. Indeed, it has been pointed out that without depression, we would lack much of the world's great tragic literature, music, and art.

In some cases, however, depression becomes something more than just the normal feelings of blues. A large number of people suffer from what psychiatrists and psychologists call "depressive illness." Depressive illness is more intense and lasts longer than common listless feelings. Sometimes a serious bout of depression begins with the loss of a loved one or a change of job. In very severe cases, there doesn't seem to be any circumstance serious enough to have caused the depression.

Researchers are not sure whether depressive illness is an aggravated form of normal depression or whether it is something different. Some psychiatrists believe that experiences occurring in early childhood may make some people more subject to depression. Some experts also believe that depression is due to disturbances in the chemistry of the brain.

Depression can show itself in many ways and with different degrees of intensity. There are a variety of possible symptoms, particularly in the milder forms of the illness.

Sometimes the key feature in depression is change. The person becomes different from the way he was before the onset of his depression. He may even become the opposite of his usual self. There are many examples: the businessman who becomes homeless, the mother who wants to harm her children and herself, and the gourmet who develops an aversion to food. Instead of seeking satisfaction and pleasure, the severely depressed person avoids it. Instead of taking care of himself, he may neglect himself and sometimes his appearance. His drive to survive gives way to suicidal wishes. His drive to succeed turns into passive withdrawal.

In general, the most obvious sign of depressive illness is a gloomy mood of sadness, loneliness, and apathy. However, if periods of deep depression seem to alternate with periods of extreme joy, this behavior may also indicate serious depressive illness.

Recalling Facts

1. According to the author, occasionally feeling depressed is
   - ☐ a. unusual.
   - ☐ b. abnormal.
   - ☐ c. normal.

2. Sometimes the key feature in depression is
   - ☐ a. change.
   - ☐ b. rejection.
   - ☐ c. indifference.

3. A severely depressed person
   - ☐ a. is dangerous.
   - ☐ b. avoids pleasure.
   - ☐ c. seeks friendship.

4. A person who is seriously depressed is usually
   - ☐ a. apathetic.
   - ☐ b. very active.
   - ☐ c. creative.

5. "Blues" as a form of music expresses
   - ☐ a. change.
   - ☐ b. the joy of success.
   - ☐ c. feelings of sadness.

Understanding the Passage

6. A gourmet suffering from depression might
   - ☐ a. argue with his friends.
   - ☐ b. develop a fear of knives.
   - ☐ c. reject favorite foods.

7. Researchers are not sure whether or not
   - ☐ a. depression and depressive illnesses are the same.
   - ☐ b. a depressed person ever thinks of suicide.
   - ☐ c. depression is a learned form of behavior.

8. A businessman who becomes severely depressed might
   - ☐ a. continue his familiar habits.
   - ☐ b. get pleasure from work.
   - ☐ c. quit his job.

9. A person who suffers from depressive illness may
   - ☐ a. imagine things which are not real.
   - ☐ b. look carelessly dressed.
   - ☐ c. not sleep well without medication.

10. The author develops this article with
    - ☐ a. specific case histories.
    - ☐ b. general examples.
    - ☐ c. surprising facts.

11 | The Dawn of Tomorrow

The Braille Institute was founded in 1919 by the late J. Robert Atkinson. He had come to Los Angeles from Montana after being blinded in a gun accident. A Brookline, Massachusetts couple, John and Mary Longyear, gave him $25,000 for the purpose of publishing raised-print books in order to improve the reading ability of the blind.

First working with his wife in the garage of their home and later with a mechanical engineer, Atkinson helped to design and build embossing plate machinery and bindery equipment that came before the publication of books.

The first publication of importance was the Braille Bible. Later he improved the printing process by a technique known as "interpointing," which enables the embossing procedure to be applied to both sides of a sheet of paper.

In 1926, he published the first book in America to use the interpoint system. Appropriately titled *The Dawn of Tomorrow*, it was an important achievement. The following year he produced the first edition of the Bible to be printed on both sides of a sheet of paper, thereby cutting both cost and bulk by about one half.

In later years other accomplishments followed: the founding of a monthly magazine for the blind, *The Braille Mirror*, the development of a Braille writer, the beginnings of legislation for passage of a White Cane Law in California, and publication of a Braille dictionary.

Atkinson realized, however, that the blind needed more than reading material. They needed rehabilitation—mobility, counseling, education, jobs, recreation, and social acceptance. Such needs, he also realized, should be organized into a program with professional guidance and continued instruction.

Over the years, the Braille Institute developed along these lines. Gradually, it increased the scope of its program and enlarged its facilities. Today it makes available more than 120 classes, services, and activities for the blind of all ages. An extensive youth program includes dozens of activities and events. A complete Braille and records library and a growing collection of magnetic tapes serve thousands of blind readers. Numerous arts and crafts classes are provided for the many sightless people who wish to develop manual skills.

Most important, however, is the trained help made available to the newly blind. Accredited teachers provide instruction in the basics of mobility and orientation, homemaking, Braille reading and writing, and the techniques of daily living. Other training that is essential to complete rehabilitation is also offered.

Recalling Facts

1. The Braille Institute was founded in
   - ☐ a. 1919.
   - ☐ b. 1926.
   - ☐ c. 1938.

2. The Braille Institute was founded by
   - ☐ a. Louis Braille.
   - ☐ b. J. Robert Atkinson.
   - ☐ c. Francisco Lucas.

3. The founder of the Institute was blinded in a
   - ☐ a. gun accident.
   - ☐ b. factory accident.
   - ☐ c. traffic accident.

4. The Braille Institute's first publication of importance was the
   - ☐ a. Declaration of Independence.
   - ☐ b. Bill of Rights.
   - ☐ c. Bible.

5. The Institute was originally financed by
   - ☐ a. private citizens.
   - ☐ b. businessmen.
   - ☐ c. the federal government.

Understanding the Passage

6. *The Braille Mirror* is
   - ☐ a. a special sensory meter for the blind.
   - ☐ b. an electronic guide stick for blind people.
   - ☐ c. a magazine for the blind.

7. "Interpointing" is a technique which allows
   - ☐ a. pictures to be printed in Braille symbols.
   - ☐ b. pages to be printed on both sides.
   - ☐ c. household appliances to be operated by the blind.

8. *The Dawn of Tomorrow* was significant because it was the first Braille book
   - ☐ a. that was not large and bulky.
   - ☐ b. sold throughout the United States.
   - ☐ c. written by a blind author.

9. We can assume that the Braille Institute offers courses in
   - ☐ a. science and technology.
   - ☐ b. home management and careers.
   - ☐ c. history and mathematics.

10. John and Mary Longyear
    - ☐ a. were the first two teachers at the Braille Institute.
    - ☐ b. traveled widely to tell people about the Institute.
    - ☐ c. helped establish the Braille Institute.

12 The Food Web

A brief look at the abundance of marine plant and animal life and how each kind relates to the others shows that the sea is much more productive than one visualizes.

Many parts of the ocean contain vast pastures of tiny, drifting plant life called phytoplankton. As in plant life on land, chlorophyll in the phytoplankton has the ability to convert the sun's energy into organic substances using simple dissolved nutrients in the surrounding water. In some places in the ocean, phytoplankton is so abundant that it changes the natural blue color of the water to shades of green, brown, or even red. Microscopic phytoplankton is the basic food that supports all aquatic life.

The next level in the food web consists of grazing animals, many also very tiny. These small creatures, known as zooplankton, range in size from simple one-celled microscopic animals to more complex and abundant forms, like fish larvae, copepods, and somewhat larger shrimplike euphausids. Free-swimming copepods, perhaps more than any other animal, eat tiny phytoplankton and convert an otherwise inaccessible food supply into a form readily available to larger animals. To indicate how abundant zooplankton is, baleen whales, the largest animals in the world, also feed on small animals, and their stomachs may often contain tons of euphausids.

Feeding on zooplankton and also on microscopic plants are the filter-feeding fishes. The gill arches of these fish have comblike filaments that strain plankton from the water. Good examples of the filter-feeders are the sardine and anchovy, which are among the smaller fishes of the sea and also the most plentiful.

Feeding on the smaller abundant fishes are larger fishes. A mackerel illustrates this level in the food web.

Finally, the top layer in the food web consists of large, carnivorous predators, like tuna, swordfish, and sharks.

The food web is an oversimplification of much more complicated processes and interactions. It serves, however, to illustrate that, at each higher level of the web, a smaller and smaller quantity of fish or shellfish is present in the ocean.

Fishery experts believe that the marine harvest can be increased at least five times to give the world a catch of 550 billion pounds. This may be achieved if we change our fishing and processing methods and our fish-eating habits to use effectively the vast numbers of marine animals not presently being caught. Turning to the sea could be the answer to many food shortage problems.

Recalling Facts

1. According to the author, phytoplankton can be found
   - ☐ a. clinging to rocks.
   - ☐ b. drifting in the water.
   - ☐ c. growing at great depths.

2. The second step in the food web consists of
   - ☐ a. phytoplankton.
   - ☐ b. filter-feeders.
   - ☐ c. zooplankton.

3. Baleen whales' stomachs contain large amounts of
   - ☐ a. euphausids.
   - ☐ b. copepods.
   - ☐ c. shrimp.

4. Among the most plentiful fish in the oceans is the
   - ☐ a. tuna.
   - ☐ b. shark.
   - ☐ c. sardine.

5. Fishery experts believe that the marine harvest can be increased
   - ☐ a. 300 percent.
   - ☐ b. 400 percent.
   - ☐ c. 500 percent.

Understanding the Passage

6. Phytoplankton is important because it
   - ☐ a. consumes pollutants in the oceans.
   - ☐ b. adds carbon dioxide to the water.
   - ☐ c. is the basic food for many fish.

7. Baleen whales are cited as examples of the
   - ☐ a. most dangerous animals in the sea.
   - ☐ b. largest animals in the world.
   - ☐ c. most endangered species in the sea.

8. The author develops this discussion according to order of
   - ☐ a. size.
   - ☐ b. importance.
   - ☐ c. time.

9. At the highest level of the food web, the
   - ☐ a. population is less dense than at lower levels.
   - ☐ b. animals are less beneficial to man.
   - ☐ c. problem of extinction becomes more serious.

10. The author implies that
    - ☐ a. the governments of the world should control sport fishing.
    - ☐ b. whale killing should not be sanctioned by any country of the world.
    - ☐ c. mankind should learn to eat lower forms of sea life.

13   The Lion's Share

Ships are taking to the highway, trucks are sprouting wings, and railroads are crossing the oceans in a transportation revolution that is sweeping the world. It's called containerization.

In this exciting new technique, products are moved from origin to destination in containers about the size of a truck trailer. The container may move first by truck and then by rail to a port where it is lifted onto a ship. At a foreign port, it is lifted off the ship and placed on wheels to go by rail or truck to the distributing warehouse. Sometimes the containers move by airplane, too.

So, a container is a ship's hold, a truck trailer, a railroad boxcar, and even an airplane fuselage. Traditional differences between land, sea, and air carriers are canceled in a highly cooperative system.

Cost savings are so great that United States and foreign port cities are quickly changing their facilities in a race for the lion's share of container shipping. Total investment in containerships in the near future is expected to reach one billion dollars. Some Japanese shippers estimate that most of their cargoes will soon be containerized.

Possibilities in this cargo revolution read like science fiction. Future containerships may travel at speeds of thirty knots or more, or about 35 miles per hour. Hydrofoil containerships may scorch the waves with speeds up to fifty miles an hour. Helicopters or other air vehicles will lift the containers from flatcars, ships, or airplanes and transport them to container yards, warehouses, or even to retail stores.

Customs and immigration methods will be simplified. Movement of containers will be governed by computers.

Present-day containers are usually eight feet wide, eight feet high, and mostly from twenty to forty feet long. Many are refrigerated and maintain the best temperature and humidity for the products they carry. They may be filled with packages of fruit, poultry, vegetables, meat, or any other product. At the point of production, the container is filled and the door is locked. From that point on, the individual packages are not handled.

Since containers are sealed by the shipper after loading, stealing and damage are almost impossible. Correct temperature in the container can be kept throughout the journey by plugging the equipment into an electric current. And because packages are not handled individually, they can be made of less expensive materials. Containerization may prove to be the goods transport system of the future.

Recalling Facts

1. The total investment in containerships in the near future will reach
   - ☐ a. $50 million.
   - ☐ b. $200 million.
   - ☐ c. $1 billion.

2. Future containerships may move at speeds of
   - ☐ a. 30 knots.
   - ☐ b. 60 knots.
   - ☐ c. 90 knots.

3. Present-day containers are usually no longer than
   - ☐ a. 20 feet.
   - ☐ b. 40 feet.
   - ☐ c. 60 feet.

4. An item mentioned that is now shipped by containerization is
   - ☐ a. machinery.
   - ☐ b. vegetables.
   - ☐ c. medicines.

5. Containerization helps to reduce
   - ☐ a. pilferage.
   - ☐ b. total weight.
   - ☐ c. packaging.

Understanding the Passage

6. The author states that containerization is more
   - ☐ a. costly than traditional shipping methods.
   - ☐ b. efficient than traditional shipping methods.
   - ☐ c. direct than traditional shipping methods.

7. According to the article,
   - ☐ a. Japan is leading the world in containerization technology.
   - ☐ b. America is spending millions of dollars in shipping research.
   - ☐ c. England was the first country to use containerization.

8. Containers usually leave their points of origin by
   - ☐ a. train.
   - ☐ b. truck.
   - ☐ c. boat.

9. When a container is carried by a plane, it is referred to as
   - ☐ a. an aileron.
   - ☐ b. a convair.
   - ☐ c. a fuselage.

10. The title of this article, "The Lion's Share," means the
    - ☐ a. amount remaining.
    - ☐ b. largest portion.
    - ☐ c. choicest piece.

14 Unsafe at Warm Temperatures

Safe handling of foods in the home should be a main concern of home-makers. Foods that are handled improperly can cause illness even though they were safe to eat when purchased or first prepared. Homemakers should be aware of the danger and know how to keep food wholesome.

Foods can become unsafe because of the growth of bacteria. Bacteria are widely distributed in the soil, water, and air. However, not all bacteria are harmful. Bacteria grow rapidly when provided with the right surroundings—food, moisture, and warmth.

Food poisoning includes both true food poisoning and bacterial food infections. True bacterial food poisoning is caused by a poison, or toxin, that is released into the food or is formed in the intestine by some bacteria. In bacterial food infection, disease-producing bacteria enter the body in contaminated food. They set up infections in the digestive tract or bloodstream after they have been swallowed.

In both cases, a large number of bacteria must be present in the food to cause illness. Large numbers of bacteria in food mean that the food has been mishandled through contamination or has been held at improper temperatures. Contamination can be a result of poor sanitary habits in food preparation. Strict cleanliness of person and surroundings is the best way to prevent the contamination of foods and the spread of food-borne illness in the home. A household member who has an infectious disease, infected cut, or skin infection should be discouraged from handling, preparing, or serving food.

Keeping foods cold slows bacterial growth and toxin production. Generally, prompt cooling and proper refrigeration of foods can hold the number of bacteria in foods to a safe level. The danger lies in holding foods for any length of time above refrigeration temperatures and below serving temperatures of hot food.

Certain foods need special care. The homemaker should always keep uncooked and cooked foods containing eggs in the refrigerator. If eggs are cracked, they should be used only in products that are to be thoroughly cooked. Unfrozen raw meat, poultry, and fish should be stored in the refrigerator. Frozen raw meat or unstuffed raw poultry should be thawed in the refrigerator. The homemaker should stuff fresh or thawed meat, poultry, or fish just before roasting.

Directions on the package of all frozen foods should be followed exactly. Heating for the specified time helps to assure that the food will be safe to eat.

Recalling Facts

1. In order to grow rapidly,
   bacteria need
   □ a. light.
   □ b. dryness.
   □ c. warmth.

2. A toxin is a
   □ a. remedy.
   □ b. preservative.
   □ c. poison.

3. Bacteria grow rapidly in
   □ a. vegetables.
   □ b. fruits.
   □ c. meats.

4. Poultry should be stuffed
   □ a. several days before
       cooking.
   □ b. several hours before
       cooking.
   □ c. just before cooking.

5. Bacteria counts are often
   high in
   □ a. stale bread.
   □ b. homemade pastries.
   □ c. cracked eggs.

Understanding the Passage

6. The author states that
   □ a. some bacteria will not
       harm people.
   □ b. very small amounts of bacteria
       can cause food poisoning.
   □ c. vegetables should be washed
       before serving.

7. Which one of the following
   should not prepare food?
   □ a. a person who has recently
       recovered from a cold
   □ b. a person who has a headache
   □ c. a person who has a finger
       infection

8. According to the author,
   frozen foods
   □ a. should be cooked longer
       than directions indicate.
   □ b. can be heated and then
       refrozen for future use.
   □ c. should be thawed according
       to printed instructions.

9. Many foods are stored at cold
   temperatures to
   □ a. prevent bacteria from
       multiplying.
   □ b. kill bacteria.
   □ c. preserve vitamin content.

10. We can conclude that
    □ a. the amount of bacteria in
        food can be controlled easily.
    □ b. fresh foods do not contain
        bacteria.
    □ c. food poisoning is a common
        illness in the United States.

15 A Fortune in Hardwoods

People in the United States pride themselves on having beautiful, attractively furnished homes. The degree of warmth and beauty in our surroundings, provided by hardwoods, is a major factor in creating this pride.

The beauty of hardwoods is important enough for today's researchers to be looking ahead. In Nevada or Oklahoma, for example, trees are a bit scarce because of climate or soil. In the Pacific Northwest where softwoods are king, the seriousness of the problem facing our future generations may be dimmed. But in Pennsylvania, Indiana, Michigan, North Carolina, and many other states, there is a serious problem.

Actually, there are two problems or situations. The first involves the ● need for educating owners of private timberlands to take better care of the nation's existing broad stands of hardwoods that cover most of our states in the northern, eastern, central, and southern regions. These trees can use a little attention. They respond to pruning, fertilization, and clearing just as corn, soybeans, and cabbage respond to plowing, cultivating, and fertilizing. And whereas the farmer gets pennies for a few plants of these crops, one good, valuable, hardwood tree can bring hundreds or thousands of dollars.

The day is gone when a person plants a hardwood grove as an invest- ● ment for grandchildren. People seem to think that is old fashioned. It dates back to the era when a person was sure that a walnut seedling, for example, wouldn't be ripe for harvesting until the next century. From data secured by researchers, a 25-year-old farmer can now plant a walnut grove and start banking money when he's sixty. With controlled harvesting, there can be a fortune in valuable hardwoods.

The second problem concerns the desirability of putting more of our finer species into the ground, just to be sure of meeting demands for a far ● larger population five decades ahead. One very notable step forward in this direction is concerted action by one of the largest single groups in the United States—the bubbling, energetic army of more than five million Boy Scouts of America. A planned program for hardwood reforestation by the Scouts was first implemented during the late sixties. The program has continued through the years to include plantings of many important species on public lands, Scout lands, and private property in hardwood growing regions.

Replacing the hardwoods that are removed for industrial reasons is recognized as being important for environmental and future security.

Recalling Facts

1. The author mentions that trees are scarce in
   - ☐ a. Kansas.
   - ☐ b. Nevada.
   - ☐ c. New Mexico.

2. Softwoods are most common in the
   - ☐ a. Midwest.
   - ☐ b. Southeast.
   - ☐ c. Pacific Northwest.

3. A vegetable mentioned in the article is
   - ☐ a. celery.
   - ☐ b. corn.
   - ☐ c. lettuce.

4. A 25-year-old farmer who plants a walnut grove can sell the wood when he is
   - ☐ a. 40.
   - ☐ b. 60.
   - ☐ c. 80.

5. How many Boy Scouts are involved in reforestation?
   - ☐ a. two million
   - ☐ b. three million
   - ☐ c. five million

Understanding the Passage

6. The article implies that
   - ☐ a. hardwood groves are more profitable today than they once were.
   - ☐ b. conifers are more resistant to disease than hardwoods.
   - ☐ c. walnut trees grow rapidly.

7. The Boy Scouts of America is mentioned as
   - ☐ a. a group that improves recreational facilities.
   - ☐ b. one of the largest organizations in the United States.
   - ☐ c. a group that is learning technical skills.

8. According to the author, people who live in North Carolina are
   - ☐ a. concerned about dwindling supplies of hardwoods.
   - ☐ b. planting large groves of softwoods.
   - ☐ c. experimenting with new strains of walnut trees.

9. The author mentions cabbage as an example of a plant that
   - ☐ a. requires little care.
   - ☐ b. responds to cultivation.
   - ☐ c. can survive harsh weather.

10. The reader can infer that
    - ☐ a. hardwoods are worth more to us than softwoods.
    - ☐ b. softwoods can be grown in any type of soil.
    - ☐ c. walnut trees grow best in damp, cool climates.

16   Viruses and Cancer

In 1911, a New York scientist succeeded in producing tumors in chickens by inoculating them with a filtrate of tumor tissue containing no cells. His experiments were the first clear demonstration of the role of a virus in one type of malignant tumor. His discovery failed to arouse much interest, however, and only a few workers continued this line of research.

But in the 1930s, two important cancer-virus discoveries were made.

First, scientists succeeded in transmitting a skin wart from a wild rabbit to domestic rabbits by cell-free filtrates. Moreover, in the domestic rabbits the warts were no longer benign, but malignant. As observed with the chickens, the filterable agent, a virus, could seldom be recovered from the malignant tumor which it had induced.

Second, in 1936, workers discovered that breast cancer in offspring of mice occurred only if the mother came from a strain noted for its high incidence of breast cancer. If the father, but not the mother, came from the high cancer line, the young ones did not develop breast cancer. When one of the simplest possibilities was explored—that something was transmitted from the mother to the young after birth—it was found that this something was a virus in the milk of the mothers. When high breast-cancer strain offspring were nursed by low breast-cancer females, the occurrence of cancer was dramatically reduced. In contrast, feeding young mice of low breast-cancer strains with milk from mice of high cancer strains greatly increased the incidence of breast cancer.

Credit for bringing the attention of investigators back to viruses is also probably due to two other discoveries in the 1950s. A scientist showed that mouse leukemia could be transmitted by cell-free filtrates. Newborn animals had to be used for these experiments.

Government scientists have succeeded in isolating from mouse leukemia tissue another agent which has produced salivary gland cancers in mice. After the agent had been grown in tissue culture, it produced many different types of tumors, not only in mice but also in rats and hamsters. This many-tumor virus removed all previous doubts about virus research in cancer. Up until then, it was believed that the few known cancer viruses could each produce only one kind of tumor in one species of animal. Now this concept was shattered, and the question of viruses as a cause of human cancer assumed new significance.

Recalling Facts

1. Filtrates of tumor tissue
   contain no
   ☐ a. viruses.
   ☐ b. cells.
   ☐ c. bacteria.

2. The first scientist to produce
   tumors with filtrates was
   ☐ a. Russian.
   ☐ b. German.
   ☐ c. American.

3. When one scientist
   transplanted a wart from one
   rabbit to another, the
   ☐ a. donor rabbit died.
   ☐ b. benign wart became
      malignant.
   ☐ c. receiver rabbit rejected
      the tissue.

4. Research with inoculations
   of filtrates was first
   conducted on
   ☐ a. rabbits.
   ☐ b. mice.
   ☐ c. chickens.

5. Doubts about virus cancer
   ended with the discovery of
   ☐ a. leukemia filtrates.
   ☐ b. malignant tumors.
   ☐ c. many-tumor viruses.

Understanding the Passage

6. The discoveries mentioned in this
   article occurred
   ☐ a. in the late 1800s and
      early 1900s.
   ☐ b. in the first quarter of the
      twentieth century.
   ☐ c. throughout the 1900s.

7. The author has arranged this
   information according to
   ☐ a. order of importance.
   ☐ b. order of interest.
   ☐ c. chronological order.

8. Government scientists proved
   that cancer
   ☐ a. occurs more often in females.
   ☐ b. can be inherited.
   ☐ c. viruses can produce different
      kinds of tumors.

9. The experimentation with breast
   cancer in mice showed that
   ☐ a. the tendency to develop
      cancer is always passed on
      to children.
   ☐ b. cancer is related to a virus in
      mother's milk.
   ☐ c. filterable viruses can be re-
      covered from induced tumors.

10. We can conclude that the search for
    the cause and cure for cancer is
    ☐ a. a slow and painstaking process.
    ☐ b. now at a standstill.
    ☐ c. primarily funded by the
       government.

17   Playing It Safe Abroad

For the great majority of Americans, travel abroad is a rich and satisfying experience. But for some it has turned out to be a nightmare.

In the last few years, hundreds of young Americans have been sent to foreign jails on drug charges. Many others have been arrested for defrauding banks, merchants, and issuers of traveler's checks. United States officials can give only limited assistance to those arrested. Penalties abroad are frequently severe and prison conditions often primitive.

Americans generally are not aware that in some countries many drug pushers are also informers for police or customs officials. Many young Americans learn about this trap the hard way.

Americans mistakenly believe foreign drug law enforcement is less stringent than in the U.S. On the contrary, prosecution of drug offenders has been intensified in countries around the world. Penalties are severe—ranging from six years in jail plus a heavy fine for possession of narcotics up to death in one country. In some countries the sentence is one to three years in a detoxification asylum, a mental hospital. Smoking marijuana can often draw the same penalties as possession or use of heroin.

Besides drugs, there are other hazards the visitor should know about. Private currency transactions with strangers, or street corner deals offering quick profits, can lead to trouble. The traveler should steer clear of black market activities, currency regulation violations, and other illegal dealings. If one is caught, the penalties are severe. Some black market dealers also prove to be police informers. If a visitor is offered an unbelievable bargain, he shouldn't believe it. It may involve stolen goods.

Laws governing cash and traveler's checks are stringent abroad. People who buy at discounts from strangers in the street can spend years in jail regretting a foolish moment. Issuers of traveler's checks, who work with local and international law enforcement authorities, have extensive security arrangements and agents in all countries. Criminal charges range from fraud and forgery to possession of stolen property and counterfeiting.

Some countries restrict purchases of certain luxury items. The visitor should beware of people offering to buy his possessions.

It isn't necessary to leave the country to get involved in the black market. For example, stolen airline tickets, sold at discount to innocent bargain hunters, can get a traveler into big trouble with the law. Airlines prosecute purchasers and sellers of stolen tickets. Travelers should make purchases only at authorized outlets.

Recalling Facts

1. In some countries people are not aware that drug pushers are
   - ☐ a. customs officials.
   - ☐ b. murderers.
   - ☐ c. informers.

2. The most severe penalty for possession of narcotics is
   - ☐ a. 10 years of hard labor.
   - ☐ b. 20 years in jail.
   - ☐ c. execution.

3. A detoxification asylum is defined in the article as a
   - ☐ a. special jail.
   - ☐ b. mental hospital.
   - ☐ c. sanatorium.

4. Some countries restrict purchases of
   - ☐ a. luxury items.
   - ☐ b. local currencies.
   - ☐ c. imported goods.

5. Before leaving the United States, one can be tempted with black market
   - ☐ a. luggage.
   - ☐ b. passports.
   - ☐ c. airline tickets.

Understanding the Passage

6. This article is primarily about
   - ☐ a. getting the best buys with foreign currency.
   - ☐ b. planning for a trip abroad.
   - ☐ c. using caution in foreign countries.

7. The article suggests that
   - ☐ a. smoking marijuana is a serious crime in some countries.
   - ☐ b. foreign jails are often filled with Americans.
   - ☐ c. traveler's checks are difficult to cash abroad.

8. The author expects that this article will appeal most to
   - ☐ a. young people who are studying law.
   - ☐ b. people who plan to travel abroad.
   - ☐ c. prospective workers in the Peace Corps.

9. For the majority of Americans, traveling abroad is usually
   - ☐ a. a gratifying experience.
   - ☐ b. a bitter disappointment.
   - ☐ c. an expensive proposition.

10. The author bases the ideas in this article on the assumption that
    - ☐ a. most foreigners try to cheat Americans.
    - ☐ b. Americans are unfamiliar with foreign laws.
    - ☐ c. customs officials are corrupt.

In the southern and central regions of California, five varieties of acorn were available to the early Indians. Acorns became their principal source of food. This was a noteworthy technological accomplishment since, in order to make the acorn edible, they first had to develop a process for leaching out the poisonous tannic acid. They ground the acorns into meal which was then filtered many times with water, either through sand or through baskets so tightly woven that the flour was not lost. In ancient campsites still remaining, we can see evidence of the amount of labor involved in reducing to meal the vast quantities of acorns needed for their subsistence. Indian women placed the acorns on any convenient flat or slightly hollowed rock and patiently ground them with stone pestles. In time, this continuing process bored holes into the stone, and, when the holes became too deep, they began on new ones. When the processing was complete, the result was a pinkish flour, which was then cooked into a gruel or mush to form the bulk of the diet. Acorns are used in California today as food by the Indians for special occasions.

Other evidences remain in California of the early presence of Indians. Pictographs painted on rocks around campsites still survive, faded but distinguishable, in some areas of southern California. Many museums display intricately fashioned stone carvings, inlaid with bone, so perfect in their execution that they would be worthy of comparison with those of the great Central American civilizations.

The ceremonial costumes used in dances and religious rites were made of the sacred eagle's feathers or other brilliant plumage from native birds. Pieces of pearly abalone shell, and sometimes the pearls themselves, were added. The Indians knew the location of every eagle's nest in each band's territory, and the nests were prized property, not to be trespassed upon. When the young eaglets began to grow feathers, they were removed from the nest, caged, and carefully nurtured in the villages or campsites. The taking of the feathers was the occasion of a night-long sacred ceremony. At dawn, the eagle was ritually slain and its feathers removed to be incorporated into the costumes. Ritual costumes were held in reverence by the people and were the sacred trust of the chieftain, to be guarded by him. Their loss or theft was the most severely punishable of crimes.

Recalling Facts

1. This article is concerned with
   the Indians of
   ☐ a. Arizona.
   ☐ b. North Dakota.
   ☐ c. California.

2. How many varieties of acorns
   were available to the Indians?
   ☐ a. three
   ☐ b. five
   ☐ c. seven

3. The poisonous substance in
   acorns is
   ☐ a. potassium cyanide.
   ☐ b. nightshade.
   ☐ c. tannic acid.

4. The flour made from
   acorns was
   ☐ a. pink.
   ☐ b. brown.
   ☐ c. yellow.

5. Museums display Indian stone
   carvings inlaid with
   ☐ a. gold.
   ☐ b. onyx.
   ☐ c. bone.

Understanding the Passage

6. The reader can assume that
   Indians valued the
   ☐ a. shells of certain turtles.
   ☐ b. feathers of birds.
   ☐ c. skins of large animals.

7. Indians were punished most
   severely for
   ☐ a. insulting the chief of a
           neighboring tribe.
   ☐ b. entering the sacred temple
           without an offering.
   ☐ c. stealing ritual costumes.

8. The author portrays the Indian
   women as
   ☐ a. religious and ceremonial.
   ☐ b. patient and hardworking.
   ☐ c. tall and very beautiful.

9. The content of this selection can
   best be described as
   ☐ a. narrative.
   ☐ b. expository.
   ☐ c. argumentative.

10. We can conclude that the artwork
    of North American Indians
    ☑ a. compares favorably with that
            of Central American Indians.
    ☐ b. was fashioned without the
            aid of metal tools.
    ☐ c. depended heavily on
            religious teachings.

19   A Firm Foundation

Many homes are now being built with foundations of pressure-treated wood walls instead of masonry block or concrete. Builders and homeowners select treated wood foundations because they want the advantages of a warm, comfortable, and more attractive house. They want a house that can be built faster in all types of weather and at less expense.

House foundations of pressure-treated wood may be used for basement or crawl space walls. These walls are framed with lumber and plywood just as are typical above-ground wood frame walls except that the lumber and plywood are pressure treated. When a basement with treated wood walls is constructed, the ground is excavated. Then gravel or crushed stone is spread over the excavation. Next, a treated wood footing plate is placed on the gravel or crushed stone fill. Finally a treated wood stud wall sheathed with treated plywood is set in place on the footing plate.

When a crawl space wall of treated wood is constructed, a trench is excavated around the perimeter of the house location. Gravel is placed in the bottom of the trench. A footing plate and wall similar to a basement wall are then set on the gravel. After the upper part of the house is framed, a concrete slab is poured in the basement and earth may be backfilled against the wood foundation wall. Crawl space walls are temporarily braced and backfilled immediately after erection.

Properly pressure-treated wood foundations are expected to last as long or longer than the average life of wood frame houses on masonry or concrete foundations.

Skyscrapers and large highway bridges are often supported by pressure-treated timber pilings. Some of these pressure treatments are unacceptable for house foundations because of their odor or capacity to soil clothing or irritate skin when touched.

Wood for house foundations pressure-treated with waterborne salt is odor free and clean and has an attractive appearance. The treatment destroys the food value of the wood, making it immune to decay by fungus or to attack by termites. A special quality mark put on each piece of lumber and plywood assures builders and owners that this material has been properly treated for residential wood foundation.

When insulation is added to a wood wall, it has one-fourth the heat loss of a conventional basement wall.

Recalling Facts

1. The least expensive foundation is made of
   - ☐ a. brick.
   - ☐ b. cement.
   - ☐ c. wood.

2. To make wood last longer, it is often treated with
   - ☐ a. oil.
   - ☐ b. salt.
   - ☐ c. silicon.

3. Underneath many foundations is a layer of
   - ☐ a. gravel.
   - ☐ b. loam.
   - ☐ c. sand.

4. A type of structure the author mentions in the article is
   - ☐ a. an A-frame house.
   - ☐ b. a skyscraper.
   - ☐ c. a modular home.

5. Some pressure treatments are unacceptable for house foundations because
   - ☐ a. of objectionable odor.
   - ☐ b. the chemicals wear off after a period of time.
   - ☐ c. the treatments are very expensive.

Understanding the Passage

6. The author implies that
   - ☐ a. wood foundations cannot be used in humid climates.
   - ☐ b. termites cannot survive in light.
   - ☐ c. cement is not poured in certain types of weather.

7. The author states that pressure-treated timber pilings
   - ☐ a. can be used for any size structure.
   - ☐ b. can be used only under single level homes.
   - ☐ c. cannot be used to support heavy structures like highway bridges.

8. The reader can infer that fungus and termites
   - ☐ a. are attracted to basement walls pressure-treated with salt.
   - ☐ b. may shorten the life of untreated wood foundations.
   - ☐ c. can cause deterioration of concrete foundations.

9. Wood that is pressure-treated
   - ☐ a. has a quality mark stamped on each piece.
   - ☐ b. is usually a dark brown color.
   - ☐ c. can support greater weights than untreated wood.

10. The reader can conclude that
    - ☐ a. many architects refuse to design houses with wooden foundations.
    - ☐ b. pressure-treated wood will be used extensively in the future.
    - ☐ c. termites will not enter painted wood.

Agony at Andersonville

Andersonville was a prison for enlisted Union soldiers during the United States Civil War. Officers, after the first few months, were confined at Macon. The first group of prisoners arrived at the camp on February 27, 1864, before the prison was completed. In the months that followed, others arrived at the rate of about 400 per day.

Overcrowding was a serious problem. By late June some 26,000 soldiers were confined in a stockade built to accommodate 10,000. By the end of July, the constant arrival of new prisoners raised the total number of soldiers being held in the prison to 31,678.

Next to overcrowding, the absence of adequate housing caused the greatest suffering. Lacking the necessary tools, the Confederates could not provide shelter for their captives. The prisoners were accordingly required to provide their own shelter. Early arrivals gathered up the lumber, logs, and branches remaining from the construction of the stockade and built rude huts. The wood supply was soon exhausted. The more resourceful Federals improvised tents, or "shebangs," from odd bits of clothing. These proved inadequate, especially during rains. Risking suffocation from cave-ins, many prisoners dug holes in the ground for protection. When it rained, these holes quickly filled with water. Hundreds of Union soldiers were without shelter of any kind against rain, sun, heat, and cold.

The daily food ration, the cause of severe dietary deficiencies, consisted of one-quarter pound of meal and either one-third pound of bacon or one pound of beef. Occasionally, peas, rice, vinegar, and molasses were provided. Food was usually issued uncooked. Prison officials had intended to cook the rations before distributing them, but the prisoners arrived before facilities had been completed. By the time a cookhouse and a bakehouse were finished in the summer of 1864, they were wholly inadequate.

The overcrowding, the inadequate shelters, the coarse, meager rations, and the poor sanitary conditions resulted in widespread disease and a high mortality rate. Altogether more than 45,000 Union soldiers had been confined in Andersonville. More than 12,000 were buried in the Andersonville cemetery. Most of the deaths were caused by diarrhea, dysentery, gangrene, and scurvy, diseases that the Confederate surgeons could not arrest because they lacked proper facilities, personnel, medical supplies, and medicines. During the prison's thirteen-month existence, more than 900 prisoners died each month. The greatest death toll on any single day occurred on August 23, 1864, when 97 prisoners died.

Recalling Facts

1. Prisoners arrived at Andersonville at the rate of four hundred per
   - ☐ a. day.
   - ☐ b. week.
   - ☐ c. month.

2. At one time, Andersonville contained more than
   - ☐ a. 25,000 men.
   - ☐ b. 50,000 men.
   - ☐ c. 75,000 men.

3. "Shebangs" were
   - ☐ a. guards.
   - ☐ b. tents.
   - ☐ c. rations.

4. Prisoners ate their food uncooked because
   - ☐ a. guards were inhuman.
   - ☐ b. cooking was unnecessary.
   - ☐ c. facilities were inadequate.

5. Andersonville was used as a prison for about
   - ☐ a. one year.
   - ☐ b. two years.
   - ☐ c. three years.

Understanding the Passage

6. Andersonville was built to accommodate
   - ☐ a. twice the number of prisoners actually detained there.
   - ☐ b. the exact number who served their sentences there.
   - ☐ c. less than one-half the number of prisoners who were held there.

7. The daily food ration for each prisoner consisted mostly of
   - ☐ a. meat.
   - ☐ b. fruit.
   - ☐ c. vegetables.

8. In this article, the author fails to mention the
   - ☐ a. location of Andersonville.
   - ☐ b. number of deaths occurring at Andersonville.
   - ☐ c. types of shelters constructed at Andersonville.

9. Confederate surgeons could not help many prisoners because the surgeons were
   - ☐ a. not licensed.
   - ☐ b. indifferent to the suffering.
   - ☐ c. inadequately equipped.

10. The author implies that Andersonville Prison was surrounded by
    - ☐ a. a large swamp.
    - ☐ b. Confederate camps.
    - ☐ c. a high wall.

21 Rems and Millirems

There are many kinds of radiation, but the one that interests environmentalists is radioactivity. Radioactivity is radiation caused by man-made changes in the structure of the atoms of which all matter is composed. Changes in the atom release tiny particles of radioactive matter that can be harmful to man and other living things. Man always has been exposed to radioactivity. It reaches us in cosmic rays from the sun and outer space. It is in the air, ground, and rocks. We have adopted units of measurement for it, which we call rems. In order to measure quantities smaller than rems, each rem is divided into one thousand parts, each of which is called a millirem.

People in different parts of the United States are exposed to natural radiation ranging from 100 to 250 millirems annually, with the average exposure about 130 millirems. In addition, the average person now receives about 77 millirems a year of man-made radiation through the use of nuclear and electromagnetic technology. Almost all man-made radiation comes from X-rays and other medical uses. Some of us receive more than others, but medical radiation accounts for about 35 percent of all radiation to which the average person is exposed.

Radiation also comes from color televisions, luminous dial watches, microwave ovens, various processes used in research and industry, nuclear plants that generate electric power, and the facilities handling the fuel for these plants.

Although nuclear power is a cheap energy source, its use is controversial. "Meltdowns" have occurred at several reactors, causing dangerous radiation leaks. And we still have inadequate methods of dealing with the radioactive waste the reactors produce. Normally, only small amounts of radioactivity are released from these reactors. Radioactivity is also released from the plants where used fuel is processed for reuse. People living within a fifty-mile radius of an operating reactor receive little radiation exposure, less than one millirem a year on the average, or less than one percent of what they receive from natural sources.

A final source of radiation is nuclear weapons. Fallout from test bombs accounts for a fraction of the man-made radiation to which we are exposed. So far only two nuclear bombs have actually been deployed. American planes dropped them on the cities of Nagasaki and Hiroshima, Japan, during World War II. The results were devastating. We all hope that nuclear weapons will never be used again.

Recalling Facts

1. Annual radiation from natural sources in the U.S. amounts to about
   - ☐ a. 50 millirems.
   - ☐ b. 130 millirems.
   - ☐ c. 270 millirems.

2. Compared with the amount of natural radiation in the atmosphere, man-made radiation is
   - ☐ a. greater.
   - ☐ b. less.
   - ☐ c. about the same.

3. Almost all man-made radiation is the result of
   - ☐ a. medical testing.
   - ☐ b. laboratory work.
   - ☐ c. nuclear power plants.

4. The use of nuclear power for energy is
   - ☐ a. widely accepted.
   - ☐ b. controversial.
   - ☐ c. unknown.

5. How far from a nuclear plant can radiation be detected?
   - ☐ a. one mile
   - ☐ b. fifty miles
   - ☐ c. ninety miles

Understanding the Passage

6. In this article, the author is primarily concerned with
   - ☐ a. natural radiation.
   - ☐ b. radioactivity.
   - ☐ c. the production of electricity.

7. According to the article, natural radiation has
   - ☐ a. always been present.
   - ☐ b. increased with the invention of nuclear power.
   - ☐ c. decreased in countries where preventive measures have been taken.

8. The author feels that nuclear weapons are
   - ☐ a. less damaging than conventional weapons.
   - ☐ b. the key to our future success in war.
   - ☐ c. things that cause immense damage.

9. Man-made radiation is caused by
   - ☐ a. creating friction between two different substances.
   - ☐ b. altering the atomic structure of substances.
   - ☐ c. changing molecules into unstable atoms.

10. The reader can conclude that
    - ☐ a. man-made radiation is a product of modern technology.
    - ☐ b. radiation poisoning is increasing around the world.
    - ☐ c. few precautions are taken with devices that cause radiation.

22 Help for the Elderly

Living in their own homes is a great desire of many older people. Some older persons with chronic conditions need regular, continuing help in preparing meals, keeping a tidy house, and personal grooming. For others, help is needed only temporarily while they recover from an illness, or while the person who usually gives care is unable to do so.

Many older people may be quite able to handle normal household tasks. They may need help with heavier chores such as washing walls, moving furniture, cleaning gutters, and taking down storm windows.

Homemaker Service in many areas provides a choice between an institution and the home for people in need of personal help. Usually sponsored by a Visiting Nurse Association, welfare department, or other social agency, Homemaker Service can be useful to all persons without regard to income, social status, or other limitation.

A Homemaker is usually a mature person with skills in home management and a basic understanding of human behavior. He or she usually has some training in simple home care of the sick. A Homemaker is not a substitute for a nurse or social worker, nor is he or she a maid.

With professional supervision by nurses or social workers, Homemakers have helped many individuals remain in familiar home surroundings. Even where older persons do not live alone, a Homemaker's services can lessen the stress on the person's usual caretaker, thereby avoiding unnecessary institutionalization.

Home Health Aides meet a variety of out-of-hospital health needs. They are sometimes part of homemaker services personnel, or part of health service teams. Before Medicare, very few health insurance programs provided coverage for Home Health Services. In recent years, many Home Health agencies have qualified to participate in the Medicare program. Studies show that physicians and patients who use Homemaker Home Health services like them. Most professionals agree that there should be more agencies offering a greater variety of in-home services.

A Homemaker-Home Health Aide is likely to be called into a home in time of crisis. The Homemaker frequently substitutes her judgment for that of the older person in his or her care. For this reason, the training, reliability, and common sense of the worker must be assured.

Many agencies and independent groups provide Homemaker-Home Health Aide service. Locally, any such service should be officially recognized by local health and welfare councils, Visiting Nurse Associations, state welfare or social service departments, and state and local health departments.

Recalling Facts

1. Homemaker Service is often sponsored by
   □ a. a Visiting Nurse Association.
   □ b. community business groups.
   □ c. departments of local governments.

2. A Homemaker may be considered a
   □ a. maid.
   □ b. social worker.
   □ c. home manager.

3. To find out more about the Homemaker Service you could contact the
   □ a. state social service office.
   □ b. yellow pages.
   □ c. local employment office.

4. The most important quality that a Home Health Aide must show is
   □ a. punctuality.
   □ b. endurance.
   □ c. good judgment.

5. The program that provides money for Home Health Services is
   □ a. Medicare.
   □ b. Social Security.
   □ c. Blue Cross.

Understanding the Passage

6. According to the author, a Homemaker must be able to
   □ a. work during many holidays.
   □ b. give medication to the sick and elderly.
   □ c. understand the personalities of people.

7. The author points out that older people with chronic illnesses
   □ a. should be hospitalized.
   □ b. can live at home if they have help.
   □ c. need the constant attention of a nurse.

8. A visiting Homemaker would never be expected to
   □ a. take down storm windows.
   □ b. administer physical therapy.
   □ c. rearrange furniture.

9. Homemaker Service is available to
   □ a. elderly people only.
   □ b. people in a low income bracket only.
   □ c. anyone who has a need for the service.

10. We can conclude that a Homemaker-Home Health Aide must be
    □ a. a college graduate.
    □ b. well trained.
    □ c. willing to travel great distances.

23   Buying a Home

When a family decides to buy a specific house, they make an offer. If the seller decides to accept the offer, the two parties discuss the terms of the contract of sale.

This contract, an agreement that is binding upon both parties, will state exactly what will be included in the purchase price.

The contract should state that it is conditional. The house must meet all local building and health codes, a termite inspection must be made, and a free and clear title must be obtainable. It also should depend on the family's ability to obtain financing for the purchase.

Some contracts to purchase real estate are not recorded. Recording the contract may be a way of preventing the seller from selling the house to another purchaser. Whether to record the contract or not will be a matter of negotiation between the buyer and the seller, subject to general practice in that area.

Assuming all has gone well in construction of a new house or that all the conditions set forth in the contract of sale for an existing house have been met, the buyer is now ready for settlement—the closing of the real estate transaction. The closing is the finalizing of the loan to finance the house or the purchase of the house.

The buyer may want an attorney to represent him at the closing. The mortgage lender may require that an attorney approved by him be used.

At final acceptance of the house the buyer should receive from the builder all guarantees and warranties that apply to the appliances, the equipment, and the structural parts of the house.

The builder should also provide a warranty, that is usually in effect for a year, on the house itself, as well as a certificate that he has paid all of his workers, subcontractors, or suppliers for work done on the house. He should also provide a waiver of lien from any worker, subcontractor, or supplier who has not yet been paid. This is a precaution for the buyer.

If the buyer does not receive the certification and waiver, he may find that someone whom the builder has not paid will be able to file a lien against the house and require payment under threat of a forced sale of the house. Thus, an attorney should review these items so that he is convinced the buyer is reasonably protected against such liens.

Recalling Facts

1. Most buyers insist that a home
   be inspected for
   □ a. water damage.
   □ b. termites.
   □ c. proper insulation.

2. Whether a contract is recorded
   or not is decided by the
   □ a. courts.
   □ b. broker.
   □ c. buyer and seller.

3. Home builders usually
   provide the buyer with
   □ a. escrow accounts.
   □ b. attorneys' fees.
   □ c. appliance guarantees.

4. A warranty on most new houses
   is effective for a period of
   □ a. one year.
   □ b. five years.
   □ c. ten years.

5. A lien against a new home
   can be filed by a
   □ a. builder.
   □ b. buyer.
   □ c. subcontractor.

Understanding the Passage

6. An attorney is most concerned with
   □ a. making sure the builder
        finishes his work before
        the bank closing.
   □ b. recording the house deed in
        the clerk's office.
   □ c. protecting the buyer against
        unpaid debts.

7. If a lien is filed against a property,
   □ a. taxes on the property increase.
   □ b. the builder of the home must
        resolve the lien.
   □ c. the owner of the home is re-
        sponsible for paying the debt.

8. A closing on property
   □ a. guarantees a property against
        defects in workmanship.
   □ b. settles all financial matters.
   □ c. establishes a contract
        between a buyer and a seller.

9. According to the author, a waiver
   of lien states that
   □ a. a worker will not file for
        back wages.
   □ b. the builder takes no respon-
        sibility for structural defects.
   □ c. the buyer has no recourse if
        someone files a lien on his
        property.

10. We can conclude that
    □ a. buying a home is a very
         informal process.
    □ b. homeowners should carry
         insurance on their property.
    □ c. written agreements give the
         buyer good protection.

24   Cool, Clear Water

Fifty million people in the United States depend upon individual water supplies. If they were asked, nearly every owner would probably say that his water was the best for miles around. This boast is common because each one has grown accustomed to the taste of his particular well water and has come to prefer that taste to all others. But many of these well owners' taste buds are deceiving them.

Surveys show that about two-thirds of the private supplies have some serious defect. Waterborne diseases, such as typhoid fever, dysentery, amebiasis, and hepatitis, continue to occur.

The owner of an individual water supply has to know more about sanitation and well construction than his city friend who depends on a municipality for such services. Fortunately, it is possible to prevent the risk of waterborne disease with proper attention to well location and construction.

Sometimes water sources are contaminated, but such sources should be avoided or sealed off in the drilling process. Treating such sources for individual water systems is not recommended.

Water systems should be disinfected after completion or after major repairs. The best disinfectant is a chlorine solution. A suitable chlorine solution can be prepared from one ounce of hypochlorite containing 70 percent available chlorine for about fifty gallons of water. Enough solution is added to fill the well and it should stand for a period of at least 24 hours.

The well should be pumped until the system is free of chlorine before the water system is used. A sample of water should be analyzed and found safe for human use. The local health department can advise a homeowner or tenant on how to arrange for this testing.

Public water supplies are treated for safety and then continuously chlorinated as an additional precaution against accidental contamination of the system.

Individual systems are usually not equipped with mechanical chlorinators and it is not recommended that they should be. The source should be safe and free of contamination as proven by bacteriological analysis. If it's unsafe, it should be corrected or abandoned. Using water from a contaminated well could be extremely hazardous to one's health.

Treatment of an unsafe source is not recommended. The system is too small and the possibility of equipment failure too great to rely on any treatment processes for safety. If a resident has a system that cannot be made safe and free from bacteriological contamination, he or she should obtain specific advice from the environmental health service immediately.

Recalling Facts

1. When well water is found to be contaminated during drilling, it should be
   - ☐ a. treated with chemicals.
   - ☐ b. sealed off.
   - ☐ c. filtered.

2. One waterborne disease mentioned in the article is
   - ☐ a. hepatitis.
   - ☐ b. scarlet fever.
   - ☐ c. pneumonia.

3. The best disinfectant for use in drinking water is
   - ☐ a. lime.
   - ☐ b. bicarbonate of soda.
   - ☐ c. chlorine.

4. Water that is treated with chemicals should not be pumped for
   - ☐ a. twelve hours.
   - ☐ b. twenty-four hours.
   - ☐ c. thirty-six hours.

5. Public water supplies are treated with chemicals
   - ☐ a. once a month.
   - ☐ b. once a year.
   - ☐ c. continuously.

Understanding the Passage

6. This article is primarily concerned with
   - ☐ a. digging a well.
   - ☐ b. finding sources of water.
   - ☐ c. treating impure water.

7. The author implies that
   - ☐ a. bacteria are tasteless and odorless.
   - ☐ b. most bacteria are harmless.
   - ☐ c. bacteria thrive where mineral deposits are heaviest.

8. The author supports the ideas in the article by presenting
   - ☐ a. several interviews.
   - ☐ b. comments by water authorities.
   - ☐ c. specific facts.

9. Before a water system is repaired,
   - ☐ a. disinfectants should be purchased.
   - ☐ b. a local health department should be notified.
   - ☐ c. a work permit should be obtained.

10. The reader can infer from the article that
    - ☐ a. mechanical chlorinators are not always necessary.
    - ☐ b. most well water is unsafe to drink.
    - ☐ c. wells should never be dug in rocky areas.

25   Scientists or Dreamers?

People the world over speak of the Space Age as beginning with the launching of the Russian Sputnik on October 4, 1957. Yet Americans might set the date back to July 1955, when the White House, through President Eisenhower's press secretary, announced that the United States planned to launch a man-made earth satellite. If the undertaking seemed bizarre to the American public at the time, to astrophysicists and some of the military the government's decision was a source of elation. After years of waiting, they had won official support for a project that promised to provide an invaluable tool for basic research in the regions beyond the upper atmosphere. Six weeks later, after a statement came from the Pentagon that the Navy was to take charge of the launching program, most Americans apparently forgot about it. It did not assume great importance again until October 1957.

Every major scientific advance has depended upon two basic elements. The first is the imaginative perception; the second is continually refined tools to observe, measure, and record phenomena that support, alter, or demolish a tentative hypothesis. This process of basic research often seems to have no immediate utility, but it is essential to progress in any field. In space exploration, the data fed back to scientists from instrumented satellites have been of utmost importance. The continuing improvement of such research opens up the prospect of greatly enlarging knowledge of the world we live in and making new applications of that knowledge.

In the decade before Sputnik, however, laymen tended to ridicule the idea of putting a man-made object into orbit around the earth. Even if the feat were possible, what purpose would it serve except to show that it could be done? As early as 1903, Konstantin Tsiolkovsky, a Russian scientist, had proved mathematically the feasibility of using the reactive force that lifts a rocket to eject a vehicle into space above the pull of the earth's gravity. Twenty years later, Romanian-born Hermann Oberth had independently worked out similar formulas. Before the 1950s, the studies of both men remained virtually unknown in the English-speaking world. Neither man had built a usable rocket to demonstrate the validity of his theories; and, as preoccupied as each man was with plans for human journeys to the moon and the planets, neither had so much as mentioned an unmanned, artificial satellite. Their basic theories, however, were proved feasible.

Recalling Facts

1. Sputnik was launched in
   - ☐ a. 1952.
   - ☐ b. 1957.
   - ☐ c. 1962.

2. To the American public, the first American launch seemed
   - ☐ a. wasteful.
   - ☐ b. overdue.
   - ☐ c. bizarre.

3. Responsibility for the American launch program was assumed by the
   - ☐ a. Army.
   - ☐ b. Navy.
   - ☐ c. Air Force.

4. Tsiolkovsky and Oberth never discussed
   - ☐ a. moon trips.
   - ☐ b. artificial satellites.
   - ☐ c. reactive forces.

5. Hermann Oberth was born in
   - ☐ a. Romania.
   - ☐ b. Poland.
   - ☐ c. Hungary.

Understanding the Passage

6. The author points out that Tsiolkovsky and Oberth never
   - ☐ a. accepted the concept of escaping the earth's gravity.
   - ☐ b. built a usable rocket to prove their theories.
   - ☐ c. had help in their laboratory work.

7. Tsiolkovsky proved that
   - ☐ a. a rocket could could be lifted into space.
   - ☐ b. solid fuel could be manufactured from known substances.
   - ☐ c. the distance to the moon was equal to the earth's axis ratio.

8. The work of Tsiolkovsky and Oberth was
   - ☐ a. published in England against their wishes.
   - ☐ b. not known for many years.
   - ☐ c. made known after their deaths.

9. The first person to prove the feasibility of rocketry was
   - ☐ a. Goddard.
   - ☐ b. Oberth.
   - ☐ c. Tsiolkovsky.

10. We can conclude that the American Space Age
   - ☐ a. began in the Kennedy Administration.
   - ☐ b. could have begun earlier than the Russian.
   - ☐ c. was based on the success of the Russian program.

The campground you enjoy may be but a small part of a large ranger district, which may vary in size from 50,000 to 500,000 acres. Its manager, a forest ranger, has a college degree in forestry or a related field and long experience as an assistant ranger. His job involves the management, development, and use of renewable forest resources—water, timber, wildlife, forage, and recreation—within his district.

Land management is a complex job that requires the ranger to be an administrator, planner, salesman, and technician. He sells timber when it is ready for harvest and insures that young trees replace those harvested. He protects the land from erosion and puts good watershed management into effect. Water flowing from national forests is a most precious resource. He makes sure that ranges are not overgrazed by big-game animals or by sheep and cattle.

The district ranger improves the wildlife habitat and cooperates with state fish and game departments to provide better fishing and hunting. He watches for the first sign of the forest's most feared enemies: disease, insects, and fire. And he counters any attack quickly and efficiently. He develops recreation areas and visits campers, hiking clubs, trail riders, skiers, and other groups making use of his district to get their suggestions for improvement. Somehow he finds time to talk to school children and to professional and civic organizations because conservation—the wise use of natural resources—is the concern of all.

These are only the highlights of the district ranger's responsibilities to the American people. He is their appointed steward and is accountable to them. But he is equally accountable to future Americans, for the forest lands that exist today must serve even more people in the years ahead.

The ranger's most important obligation, then, is clear. He must intensify management and development so that each resource—water, timber, wildlife, forage, recreation—will produce forest products and services at a high level of supply. This must be done without harming the land's ability to produce, now or in the future. This limited quantity of land must be protected.

This is the Forest Service's policy of managing forest land for multiple use and sustained yield. It has proved to be good conservation. It is the means by which the Forest Service and the district ranger will continue to provide greater services to a growing nation through the wise use of forest resources.

Recalling Facts

1. The manager of a ranger district is trained as a
   - ☐ a. district manager.
   - ☐ b. forest ranger.
   - ☐ c. animal manager.

2. Which one of the following would be an average-sized district?
   - ☐ a. 10,000 acres
   - ☐ b. 25,000 acres
   - ☐ c. 100,000 acres

3. The manager of a district is directly responsible to
   - ☐ a. the government.
   - ☐ b. his superiors.
   - ☐ c. the people.

4. Which one of the following is *not* a renewable forest resource?
   - ☐ a. minerals
   - ☐ b. timber
   - ☐ c. recreation

5. One of the greatest threats to the continuation of the range is
   - ☐ a. overgrazing.
   - ☐ b. disease.
   - ☐ c. drought.

Understanding the Passage

6. According to this selection, the forest's most feared enemies are
   - ☐ a. the result of natural processes.
   - ☐ b. the product of man's carelessness.
   - ☐ c. man-made and nature-created.

7. This selection takes the form of
   - ☐ a. a short story.
   - ☐ b. an essay.
   - ☐ c. a description.

8. The intent of the author is to
   - ☐ a. outline the work of district managers.
   - ☐ b. portray the district managers as law enforcement officials.
   - ☐ c. discuss the sequence of steps taken to become a district manager.

9. The Forest Service's policy for good conservation is
   - ☐ a. preserving natural attractions and caring for campgrounds.
   - ☐ b. improving the wildlife habitat and protecting natural resources.
   - ☐ c. managing forest land for multiple use and sustained yield.

10. We may infer from this selection that district managers are
    - ☐ a. trained by the Department of Agriculture.
    - ☐ b. involved mostly with the supervision of campgrounds.
    - ☐ c. responsible for all facets of land management.

For many years, Antarctica was thought to be only an archipelago whose islands were tied together above sea level by ice. It was thought to be made up of two small subcontinents—East Antarctica, the larger, and West Antarctica, containing the Antarctic Peninsula. The two continents were supposed to be separated by a large trough, below sea level, that connected the Ross and Weddell Seas.

Geophysical studies have now revealed a fairly complete picture of the Antarctic landform below its ice cover. We know now that West Antarctica is connected to the main part of the continent by a chain of mountains well above sea level, though largely buried by ice and snow. The bedrock of much of East Antarctica appears to be above sea level. Some of it, in high ranges of the Transantarctic Mountains, is far above sea level.

Whether mineral wealth lies hidden by the vast ice sheets is unknown. No more than two percent of the continent is actual rock outcrop and much of this small and probably unrepresentative sample has yet to be visited by geologists. Certainly no deposits rich enough to be economically useful have been found.

Geologists now know that the ice-buried rocks of the Antarctic are similar to rocks of the other continents of the world. Minor amounts of potentially valuable minerals have been reported. The presence of petroleum has been speculated upon by several geologists, but none has yet been found. Low-grade deposits of coal are widespread, especially in the Transantarctic Mountains, but there has been no attempt at exploitation. Even if rich mineral deposits were to be found in Antarctica, the cost of removal from this remote and inhospitable land would be exorbitant.

Interpretation of continental structure is an important objective of any extensive geologic investigation. Yet except for the earth's ocean basins, no area the size of Antarctica is so geologically unknown. With 98 percent of the continent covered by ice, it is extremely difficult to decipher the continent's general structure. Geologists determine geologic structure by studying rock outcrops, and many of these are small and widely separated. No outcrops are known in the vast interior of East Antarctica.

Working out the continental structure of Antarctica is analogous to learning that of the entire United States from studies of a few scattered counties in California and mountain ranges scattered at irregular intervals across the country.

Recalling Facts

1. Little is known about Antarctica's
   - ☐ a. climate.
   - ☐ b. landform and size.
   - ☐ c. mineral wealth.

2. How much of Antarctica is covered by ice?
   - ☐ a. 52 percent
   - ☐ b. 76 percent
   - ☐ c. 98 percent

3. Antarctica is made up of
   - ☐ a. several islands.
   - ☐ b. two subcontinents.
   - ☐ c. connected land masses.

4. In Antarctica, petroleum
   - ☐ a. is common.
   - ☐ b. cannot form.
   - ☐ c. may be present.

5. Low-grade deposits of coal have been found in Antarctica's
   - ☐ a. valleys.
   - ☐ b. coastline.
   - ☐ c. mountains.

Understanding the Passage

6. This article is concerned primarily with the
   - ☐ a. exploration for minerals in Antarctica.
   - ☐ b. geological composition of Antarctica.
   - ☐ c. establishment of Antarctica's geophysical laboratory.

7. The author implies that Antarctica
   - ☐ a. is a group of separate islands.
   - ☐ b. consists of two separate islands.
   - ☐ c. is really one large island.

8. The author suggests that geologists
   - ☐ a. study rocks with little difficulty in Antarctica.
   - ☐ b. find ice and snow to be a problem in rock study.
   - ☐ c. have never tried to extract minerals from Antarctica.

9. California is mentioned to
   - ☐ a. illustrate the type of rock found in Antarctica.
   - ☐ b. show the difficulty in mapping the structure of Antarctica.
   - ☐ c. provide an example of uniform climate.

10. We may conclude that
    - ☐ a. Antarctica will someday supply the world's mineral needs.
    - ☐ b. geophysical studies of Antarctica are now complete.
    - ☐ c. controversy exists on the geological composition of Antarctica.

28 Marine Mineral Resources

In recent years, several billion barrels of petroleum have been obtained from beneath the floors of the continental shelves that fringe the United States. This yield was the result of exploration based mainly on geological and geophysical data from subsea structures. Tin-bearing and iron-bearing sands, sulfur, gravel, and cement materials are now being produced from offshore areas in many parts of the world. These resources are all mined from the sea floor, but salt and magnesium are extracted from the sea water itself. Diamonds and gold are now being sought on the continental shelves. Mining operations are under way, and profitable recovery has been reported in some areas.

Several kinds of useful minerals from extensive low-grade deposits are likely to serve as resources in the future. Phosphorite, potentially useful as fertilizer, occurs on the continental shelves in nodules or as coating on rocks. Large areas of the deep ocean floor are literally paved with manganese nodules. These are rounded black stones that contain not only manganese but other useful metals. At present these metals cannot be obtained from the nodules as economically as they can from deposits now being mined on land, but the nodules could provide an important resource if the land deposits were used up.

Mining claims may not be filed for mineral deposits on the continental shelves as they may for ores on public land. An international convention has given each country the exclusive right to exploit minerals off its coast out to a water depth of 200 meters and, beyond that limit, to where the depth of the water above permits the exploitation of the natural resources. In the United States the mineral resources of the outer part of our shelves are leased by the federal government under the Outer Continental Shelf Lands Act of 1953. Those of the inner part are leased by the adjacent states. For most states, the boundary between the inner and outer parts of the shelves is defined as those lying three miles from shore. Whoever wishes to explore for marine minerals obtains a prospecting permit from the federal government or state having jurisdiction. The person then bids for a lease and pays royalties to the government if minerals are found. Because the continental shelves are equal in area to one-fifth of the territory of the United States, they will become an increasingly important source of minerals in the future.

Recalling Facts

1. How many barrels of petroleum have been extracted from the ocean floor in recent years?
   □ a. one million
   □ b. several billion
   □ c. none

2. The scientist who interprets the undersea structure is called a
   □ a. geologist.
   □ b. biologist.
   □ c. minerologist.

3. Which one of the following metal ores is not mined beneath the sea?
   □ a. silver
   □ b. gold
   □ c. tin

4. Which one of the following precious stones is being mined offshore?
   □ a. sapphires
   □ b. emeralds
   □ c. diamonds

5. Phosphorite is potentially useful as
   □ a. food.
   □ b. jewelry.
   □ c. fertilizer.

Understanding the Passage

6. The discovery of mineral deposits offshore has
   □ a. provoked legal mining claims.
   □ b. incited international disagreements.
   □ c. prompted an international mining convention.

7. The author uses the word "exploit" to mean
   □ a. take advantage of without regard for others.
   □ b. use wisely and efficiently.
   □ c. use carelessly and foolishly.

8. The use of the outer parts of our ocean floor shelves is controlled by
   □ a. private mining firms which specialize in ocean technology.
   □ b. a special committee of the United Nations.
   □ c. a department of the federal government.

9. The article states that
   □ a. state governments have some say in underwater mining.
   □ b. minerals in the ocean's floor are insignificant.
   □ c. feeding the hungry of the world is a hope of geologists.

10. We can conclude that
   □ a. continental shelves will become a source of minerals.
   □ b. the United States will become a leader in underwater mining.
   □ c. the quality of minerals will improve through the years.

29 Asthma

Few people can easily forget the sight of a child or an adult who is having an asthma attack. The victim breathes rapidly and gasps for air. Spasms of coughing wrack his body. Wheezing sounds may be so loud that they can be heard across the room. In fact, the asthmatic acts and feels much like a drowning person struggling for air.

Asthma is a noncontagious disease of the lungs. Yet it is a very common illness. Nearly nine million Americans, young and old, are asthmatics. Many begin having attacks in early childhood and continue to have them throughout their lives. Others seem to "outgrow" their asthma by the time they reach adolescence. Usually, however, untreated asthma gets worse, not better.

Repeated attacks of forced breathing may cause permanent damage of air passages. However, with proper medical care, most asthma patients can live normal, productive, and active lives.

Asthma is not usually fatal, although as many as 3,000 persons in the United States do die from this disease each year. However, because of its chronic and unpredictable nature, it is very weakening.

In a large number of asthmatics, aspirin will set off an asthma attack, although the individuals are not really allergic to it. Asthmatics should, therefore, avoid the use of aspirin or aspirin-containing products.

Geography, climate, and work may play a role if an asthmatic's attacks are related to specific allergens or complicated by infections. There is growing evidence, too, that air pollution, because of irritating effects, plays an important part in asthma attacks. One recent study showed that asthmatics are prone to have more attacks when there are high levels of sulfur dioxide, a common pollutant, in the air. However, a drastic change of location should not be made without the guidance of a doctor.

Emotional stresses can trigger attacks in many asthmatic patients, both children and adults. Emotional factors in asthma seem to be more important as minor factors than as major causative ones. In any event, they should not be ignored. The mental suffering and loss of energy and confidence that result from repeated asthma attacks can hinder the normal development of children.

In those cases where infection plays a major role, careful attention to general health and protection from such factors as chilling and bad weather are helpful. Avoidance of other persons suffering from colds and vaccination against influenza during the winter season is also advised.

*Reading Time*_____ *Comprehension Score*_____ *Words per Minute*_____

Recalling Facts

1. An asthmatic feels like someone who is
   - ☐ a. feverish.
   - ☐ b. sleeping.
   - ☐ c. drowning.

2. Asthma is considered a disease of the
   - ☐ a. bronchial tubes.
   - ☐ b. lungs.
   - ☐ c. esophagus.

3. How many million Americans are asthmatics?
   - ☐ a. 9
   - ☐ b. 12
   - ☐ c. 15

4. Asthma is classified as
   - ☐ a. fatal.
   - ☐ b. contagious.
   - ☐ c. chronic.

5. How many people in the U.S. die of asthma annually?
   - ☐ a. 1,000
   - ☐ b. 2,000
   - ☐ c. 3,000

Understanding the Passage

6. After reading this article, one should be able to
   - ☐ a. give emergency treatment to an asthmatic.
   - ☐ b. diagnose asthma with accuracy.
   - ☐ c. understand some causes of asthma.

7. The author advises that an asthmatic with a headache should *not*
   - ☐ a. breathe deeply.
   - ☐ b. go to sleep.
   - ☐ c. take aspirin.

8. The author states that
   - ☐ a. childhood asthma lasts through adulthood.
   - ☐ b. asthma is a childhood disease.
   - ☐ c. attacks of forced breathing can damage breathing passages.

9. The article strongly suggests that
   - ☐ a. a person with severe asthma should immediately move to a dry climate.
   - ☐ b. sulphur dioxide can cause asthma to develop.
   - ☐ c. asthmatic attacks can be induced by allergies.

10. A person with asthma should not
   - ☐ a. travel to large cities with poor air quality.
   - ☐ b. engage in physical exercise programs.
   - ☐ c. take walks during winter months.

Thousands of homes, businesses, and industries on the flood plains suffer some degree of flood loss every year. Huge losses are inflicted on structures, equipment, and stored products in both urban and rural areas. And the amount of these losses is growing.

Our rapid growth of population has increased the pressure to use lands that are close to the centers of growth. Consequently, many flood plains have been developed when they should have been left as open space for recreation, agriculture, or for other uses that flooding would not seriously damage.

Flood control programs have provided partial protection for a large number of flood hazard areas, but it is not possible to protect all areas. The size of the problem measured both physically and financially is too big. And flood control isn't physically practical for some areas.

Floodwaters affect buildings in various ways. A horizontal force acts to crush the structural walls. Water pressure can force water through cracks, small openings, and even through some types of walls, thus causing the buildings to leak. The buoying effect of the water may lift the building enough to permit the power of the moving water to slide the structure from its foundation. And erosion by swiftly flowing water tends to undermine the foundation itself.

Flood proofing is an action you can take to make your own buildings watertight and to adjust the contents or location of your buildings to minimize flood losses. It also includes actions to protect roads, streets, lawns, fields, livestock, and your family from floods.

Flood proofing is especially effective in areas where the depths of floodwater are not great. It is also most effective where the floodwater velocities are slow and for areas that are flooded for only short periods.

You may think that you do not have a flood problem because there is a flood control dam upstream or because the river or stream channel near you has been enlarged. Few flood control projects provide complete protection. You can usually increase your individual protection by flood proofing your buildings and property.

Maybe your activities require buildings located upon the banks of rivers and streams. These may be pumphouses for water supply, warehouses for temporary storage of goods being shipped by barge or boat, or buildings for water-related recreation. Buildings for such activities can be flood proofed to provide a reasonable degree of protection from the floods that you should expect.

*Reading Time*_____ *Comprehension Score*_____ *Words per Minute*_____ 73

Recalling Facts

1. The author feels that flooding does not seriously damage
   □ a. agricultural land.
   □ b. residential land.
   □ c. commercial land.

2. Flood proofing is the responsibility of
   □ a. the individual.
   □ b. the community.
   □ c. civil defense.

3. The buoying effect of flood waters
   □ a. crushes buildings.
   □ b. raises buildings.
   □ c. undermines buildings.

4. What has contributed to the development of lands that should have been left as open space?
   □ a. population growth
   □ b. federal controls
   □ c. farm expansion

5. Flood proofing is an action that makes buildings
   □ a. more secure.
   □ b. watertight.
   □ c. totally safe.

Understanding the Passage

6. Flood control programs so far have been
   □ a. completely successful in protecting flood hazard areas.
   □ b. moderately successful in protecting centers of growth.
   □ c. unsuccessful in densely populated areas.

7. In a flood, buildings are affected most by
   □ a. moving water that carries buildings many miles away.
   □ b. objects that are thrown against buildings.
   □ c. a combination of forces that work in unison.

8. Flood proofing would be most needed
   □ a. in low areas near bodies of water.
   □ b. in urban areas with civil defense operations.
   □ c. on tracts of land well removed from bodies of water.

9. Toward the person who feels confident of his safety because there is a flood control dam upstream, the writer is
   □ a. mildly critical.
   □ b. very complimentary.
   □ c. bitterly sarcastic.

10. The author avoids
    □ a. citing examples of flood devastation in this country.
    □ b. advising people to flood proof their property.
    □ c. mentioning places where flood dangers are greatest.

31 The Value of Gold

Throughout history, gold has been a precious material, eagerly sought and cherished. It was probably the first metal to be mined because it is beautiful and imperishable, and because beautiful objects can be made from it—even with primitive tools. The amount of gold known to ancient peoples probably totaled not much more than the amount produced each year by the world's largest gold mine located in the Witwatersrand district of South Africa. Hoards of gold discovered by archaeologists in Greece, Scythia, and Egypt, as well as the gold from Indian treasuries in Mexico and Peru, represented years of patient collection of small quantities from streams and veins, often by slave labor.

The intrinsic value of gold has always been known, even before gold was used in coinage. It remains the only universally recognized standard of value in international monetary exchange. Most of the world's refined gold is absorbed by governments and central banks to provide backing for paper currency. But the amount of gold used in the arts and in industry is increasing. In addition to its use for jewelry, decorative finishes, and dentistry, its special properties have led to many applications in modern science and technology. Surface coatings of gold protect earth satellites from heat and corrosion, and certain electrical components and circuits of spacecraft are made of gold when extreme reliability is required.

Gold was first produced in the United States from the southern Appalachian region, beginning about 1792. These deposits, though rich, were relatively small and were quickly depleted. The discovery of gold at Sutter's Mill in California sparked the gold rush of 1849-50. Hundreds of mining camps sprang to life as new deposits were discovered. As a result, the production of gold increased rapidly.

During World War I and for some years thereafter, annual production declined to about two million ounces. When the price of gold was raised in 1934 to $35 an ounce, production increased rapidly. Shortly after the start of World War II, gold mines were closed and the government did not permit them to reopen until 1945. Since then, the production of gold has not exceeded two million ounces a year.

The largest producing gold mine in the United States is the Homestake Mine in South Dakota, which yields about 575,000 ounces of gold each year. Other mines throughout the world produce even larger amounts of this highly prized and eagerly sought yellowish mineral.

Recalling Facts

1. The world's largest gold mine is located in
   - ☐ a. southern France.
   - ☐ b. North Dakota.
   - ☐ c. South Africa.

2. Indian treasures of gold have been found in
   - ☐ a. Peru.
   - ☐ b. Chile.
   - ☐ c. Argentina.

3. Most of the world's refined gold is used for
   - ☐ a. currency backing.
   - ☐ b. circulating coinage.
   - ☐ c. expensive jewelry.

4. Surface coatings of gold protect earth satellites from
   - ☐ a. radiation.
   - ☐ b. heat.
   - ☐ c. discovery.

5. Gold was first mined in the United States during the
   - ☐ a. late 1700s.
   - ☐ b. early 1800s.
   - ☐ c. middle 1800s.

Understanding the Passage

6. The two million ounces of gold produced during World War I represented
   - ☐ a. a decrease in the amount of gold on the market.
   - ☐ b. an increase in the amount of gold in circulation.
   - ☐ c. a stabilization in the amount of gold mined.

7. This selection suggests that
   - ☐ a. the United States is the largest producer of gold in the world.
   - ☐ b. governments control the production of gold.
   - ☐ c. ancient peoples mined gold in large quantities.

8. The author arranges information primarily in order of
   - ☐ a. time.
   - ☐ b. use.
   - ☐ c. importance.

9. To develop the ideas in this article, the author uses
   - ☐ a. factual description.
   - ☐ b. arguments and proof.
   - ☐ c. personal opinions.

10. We can conclude that
    - ☐ a. gold supplies are rapidly coming to an end.
    - ☐ b. dentistry is using more gold now than ever before.
    - ☐ c. gold has always been considered valuable.

32   A Shaft of Vermont Granite

The preservation of Washington's birthplace was the work of many people and groups. In 1859, John E. Wilson, owner of most of the Popes Creek-Bridges Creek land, deeded to the Commonwealth of Virginia a right-of-way through his farm to the birthsite and the Washington family burying ground. He also deeded one-half acre of land near the burying ground and about one acre near the birthsite.

In 1882, the Commonwealth of Virginia gave to the United States of America its holdings at the birthsite and burying ground. In 1879, an act of Congress approved the construction of a monument to mark the birthsite. The acquisition of the necessary ground and right-of-way had already been authorized. In 1883, Mr. and Mrs. John E. Wilson sold to the United States nearly twelve acres of land surrounding the birthsite. They also sold nine acres constituting a right-of-way connecting the birthsite, the family burying ground, and the Potomac River near the mouth of Bridges Creek.

Although Congress had authorized the construction of a monument to mark the birthsite, fifteen years passed before the shaft of Vermont granite was erected. It was a time in our nation's history when historical conservation was crowded into the background in favor of more materialistic aims.

In the 1920s, a group of women became interested in the old Washington plantation. They wanted more than a granite monument to memorialize the site where our first President was born. On February 23, 1923, under the able leadership of Mrs. Josephine Wheelright Rust, they organized the Wakefield National Memorial Association. Their main objective was to restore the Wakefield plantation and make it a shrine for all people. The date set for completion of the task was 1932, the 200th anniversary of Washington's birth.

Shortly after the Wakefield National Memorial Association was incorporated in 1924, its members raised funds for acquiring land between the birthsite and the Washington family burial ground. They persuaded John D. Rockefeller, Jr., to purchase 273 acres of the old Wakefield plantation and transfer it to the United States government. By an act of Congress, the Association was given authority to construct a house at Wakefield like the one built by Augustine Washington. In 1929, the Association acquired additional land, and two years later donated its holding at Wakefield to the United States. Thus, through the hard work of many interested and concerned citizens, a permanent memorial to George Washington was established.

Recalling Facts

1. The owner of most of the land around the Washington homestead was
   - ☐ a. a farmer.
   - ☐ b. an industrialist.
   - ☐ c. a politician.

2. Land around the Washington homestead was first deeded to Virginia in the
   - ☐ a. 1820s.
   - ☐ b. 1850s.
   - ☐ c. 1880s.

3. Congress enacted legislation to build a
   - ☐ a. tourist center.
   - ☐ b. monument.
   - ☐ c. shrine.

4. Land around the Washington birthplace eventually reached as far as
   - ☐ a. the Potomac River.
   - ☐ b. Washington, D.C.
   - ☐ c. the Virginia border.

5. Interest in the old Washington plantation was renewed in the
   - ☐ a. 1920s.
   - ☐ b. 1940s.
   - ☐ c. 1950s.

Understanding the Passage

6. From the article, the reader can infer that
   - ☐ a. Congress often acts slowly on legislation.
   - ☐ b. materialistic aims often impede progress in other areas.
   - ☐ c. the Washington plantation is now a profitable tourist attraction.

7. The Washington plantation has been preserved mostly through the efforts of
   - ☐ a. the federal government.
   - ☐ b. concerned citizens.
   - ☐ c. Virginia businesspeople.

8. According to the article, most people think of Washington as
   - ☐ a. the first President of the United States.
   - ☐ b. a great Revolutionary War general.
   - ☐ c. a patriotic American.

9. The Wakefield National Memorial Association restored the Washington home over a period of
   - ☐ a. three years.
   - ☐ b. nine years.
   - ☐ c. twelve years.

10. The author mentions that John D. Rockefeller, Jr.,
    - ☐ a. sponsored legislation to help the restoration committee.
    - ☐ b. contributed large sums of money for the restoration.
    - ☐ c. purchased a large tract of land for the restoration committee.

33　Withdrawal Syndromes

Detecting drug abuse is not a simple matter. A youngster who wears his hair differently, alters his manner of dress, and begins to associate with new friends is probably undergoing changes in his attitude and lifestyle. Such changes, however, are often seen in the adolescent years and do not always mean that drugs are being abused.

It may be helpful for a parent to become acquainted with the most usual signs of the physical and behavioral effects of certain drugs. At the same time, parents must understand that such signs are by no means conclusive. They may indicate physical or emotional disorders.

Drugs most often abused are narcotics, sedatives, stimulants, and hallucinogens. They all have either a depressant or excitatory effect on the central nervous system of the body. Persons under the influence of narcotics, such as heroin, usually are drowsy and apathetic. They have little interest in what is going on around them. If, however, they have been taking the drug on a regular basis, tolerance can reduce the severity of such symptoms.

When a person has been taking heroin or another narcotic long enough to develop physical dependence, a typical syndrome appears from eight to twelve hours after the last dose. The most common signs, mild at first and becoming more and more obvious as time goes on, include a running nose, watery eyes, yawning, and perspiring. During the second day following withdrawal, stomach cramps, vomiting, diarrhea, and muscle spasms causing uncontrollable kicking and twitching are usually experienced.

Although not very dangerous, the withdrawal period for a narcotic-dependent person can be highly discomforting and painful. Medical help should be sought to relieve distress.

Sedative drugs, such as barbiturates, also have a depressant effect on the central nervous system. But like alcohol, with which they have a cross-tolerance, they can cause a person to be giddy, talkative, and agitated during the early intoxication state. These signs are displaced by grogginess, drowsiness, and sleep as time goes on.

Severe intoxication does not normally occur if the sedative is taken in small prescribed doses. And it is only through taking larger amounts often over a long period of time that physical dependence develops. If that happens, however, it is essential that the person who discontinues use be hospitalized and observed closely. Withdrawal from barbiturates in such a case can be dangerous and even fatal unless expertly controlled.

Recalling Facts

1. One symptom of drug abuse is a
   - ☐ a. change of hair style.
   - ☐ b. rejection of former friends.
   - ☐ c. lack of interest in surroundings.

2. A withdrawal syndrome follows a dose of narcotics in as little time as
   - ☐ a. four hours.
   - ☐ b. eight hours.
   - ☐ c. sixteen hours.

3. One of the first signs of withdrawal is
   - ☐ a. vomiting.
   - ☐ b. watery eyes.
   - ☐ c. twitching.

4. Withdrawal from heroin is often
   - ☐ a. fatal.
   - ☐ b. unnoticeable.
   - ☐ c. painful.

5. Detecting drug abuse is
   - ☐ a. quite easy.
   - ☐ b. difficult.
   - ☐ c. usually impossible.

Understanding the Passage

6. According to the author, drugs most often abused
   - ☐ a. affect the heart and lungs.
   - ☐ b. affect the central nervous system.
   - ☐ c. reduce the flow of blood to the arms and legs.

7. Information in the article suggests that
   - ☐ a. a physical dependence on drugs develops gradually.
   - ☐ b. drugs can cause genetic imbalance.
   - ☐ c. a person who takes drugs often suffers from insomnia.

8. Barbiturates usually cause a person to become
   - ☐ a. introspective.
   - ☐ b. argumentative.
   - ☐ c. talkative.

9. The author points out that adolescents
   - ☐ a. often change their life-styles for no apparent reason.
   - ☐ b. take drugs to get attention from their parents.
   - ☐ c. reject the political views of adults.

10. Symptoms of drug abuse are most difficult to detect in
   - ☐ a. very young children.
   - ☐ b. long-time users.
   - ☐ c. elderly people.

34 The American Tradition of Camping

Every year more people enjoy the National Forests and National Grasslands—187 million acres of the best of our country's magnificent outdoors. Annually, more than 40 million persons use the 5,500 developed campgrounds on these public lands. Camping accounts for over one-quarter of all recreational activities in the National Forests and National Grasslands. These areas now host ten times as many campers as fifteen years ago, and the number of visitors is still rising.

The use of forests for many purposes is traditional with a people for whom the outdoors has always been close at hand. Our forefathers hunted and fished forest lands and used forest trees for building. Often in their travels, though more from necessity than for fun, they camped deep in the woods.

In later years, but still long before the establishment of the National Forests, Americans were finding relaxation and challenge in camping, fishing, hunting, and otherwise exploring the nation's backcountry.

How and why do all these folks find fun pitching camp and roughing it in the woods?

Many of them hunt. One-third of the big game animals in the United States inhabit the National Forests: the unposted, happy hunting grounds of our nation. Other campers enjoy some of the finest fishing in the country, along thousands of miles of clear stream and at natural impounded lakes located in the National Forests.

Campers also go hiking, swimming, boating, waterskiing, motorscooting, and horseback riding. They pick berries, collect rocks, watch birds, and photograph wild flowers, wild animals, the superb scenery, and one another. They also spend time contemplating, socializing, and singing around the evening campfire.

Obviously there's no simple explanation for the strong attraction Americans feel for the outdoors. Each person comes for reasons special to him, and possibly just to be in the open, living close to the land. Fortunately, for a nation of people strongly drawn to the outdoors, open space and forest recreation, even in this age of urban sprawl, are still readily available and easily reached.

The beginning camper may need information to get started. Good maps are useful to the camper in planning trips and are necessary when traveling unfamiliar roads. In addition to showing National Forests, many atlases and roadmaps distributed by service stations and state highway departments indicate the location of recreation areas in National Forests, as well as recreation areas on other federal and state public lands and on private lands.

Recalling Facts

1. According to the article, how many people use the National Forests annually?
   ☐ a. 5 million
   ☐ b. 20 million
   ☐ c. 40 million

2. Today the forests host how many times more people than 15 years ago?
   ☐ a. 10
   ☐ b. 20
   ☐ c. 25

3. The number of developed campgrounds on public lands exceeds
   ☐ a. 500.
   ☐ b. 1,000.
   ☐ c. 5,000.

4. The first item for the camper who is planning a trip is a
   ☐ a. compass.
   ☐ b. map.
   ☐ c. knife.

5. Which one of the following activities is not mentioned in the article?
   ☐ a. motorscooting
   ☐ b. berry picking
   ☐ c. bicycling

Understanding the Passage

6. The woodlands have been a useful asset to America since the
   ☐ a. first people began to move west.
   ☐ b. National Forest Service was founded.
   ☐ c. earliest colonies were established.

7. If 900 big game animals live in the United States, how many occupy the forests?
   ☐ a. 300
   ☐ b. 450
   ☐ c. 600

8. The strong attraction to the outdoors is based on
   ☐ a. each person's own special needs.
   ☐ b. extensive advertising by the U. S. Forest Service.
   ☐ c. the need for strenuous physical exercise.

9. This selection is most likely taken from
   ☐ a. a documentary on the uses of federal lands.
   ☐ b. a book dealing with government land purchases.
   ☐ c. an article promoting the use of National Forests.

10. The reader can conclude that
    ☐ a. most National Forests are closed during winter months.
    ☐ b. wild animals are sometimes a problem in National Forests.
    ☐ c. many National Forests and Grasslands may be used without damage.

35

The Ocean as a Storehouse

Traditionally, the fishery scientist has conducted research from a vessel that is really a floating platform. Instruments can be towed or sent down from this platform to record information on the environment. Such information might include salinities, water temperatures, strength and direction of water currents, and the amounts and types of plankton. Nets or other fishing gear can be used on the surface or at various depths down to the ocean bottom. From the fish and shellfish caught, life history studies can be made. Using many indirect techniques, like tagging, the size of a population of fish and shellfish could be estimated.

In the laboratory, many things can be done. The age of fish can be determined from rings on scales or from ear stones known as otoliths. Blood serum analysis can be made to sort out the different races that often make up a species.

Using knowledge of the age and size of fish, as well as the catch records of fishing vessels and statistical records of the annual catch of a species over a period of time, signs of overfishing can be detected.

Many of these traditional research techniques have been refined, and much valuable biological information has been gathered. Fishery research, however, is still in its infancy. As more and more attention is given to the ocean as a storehouse of food, newer and better tools are being developed for fishery research.

An important aim of fishery biological and oceanographic research is to determine the point at which commercial or sport fishermen can catch fish or shellfish, year after year, without destroying the ability of a species to reproduce and sustain itself. Individuals of a species will die. But before they die, fishermen can and should catch that surplus that may safely be removed.

Biologists have coined the phrase "maximum sustainable yield" to denote this equilibrium or balance that needs to be achieved if successful fisheries are to be conducted indefinitely. When fishermen take more than the permissible surplus, the numbers or weight of fish available to fishermen will decline. This is known as overfishing, and eventually the number of individuals in a resource is reduced to a level where fishermen find it unprofitable to fish. All of this is not as simple as it appears. An ideal equilibrium is never maintained for a very long period of time. Every farmer, fish culturist, or horticulturist knows this fact.

Recalling Facts

1. Fishery scientists usually conduct research from
   - ☐ a. submarines.
   - ☐ b. floating platforms.
   - ☐ c. bathospheres.

2. Otoliths are actually
   - ☐ a. ear stones.
   - ☐ b. fish scales.
   - ☐ c. shellfish.

3. The rings on fish scales can reveal the fish's
   - ☐ a. origin.
   - ☐ b. eating habits.
   - ☐ c. age.

4. Fishery research is
   - ☐ a. just beginning.
   - ☐ b. very advanced.
   - ☐ c. highly sophisticated.

5. Fishery scientists are most concerned with
   - ☐ a. water pollution.
   - ☐ b. overfishing.
   - ☐ c. extinction of rare species.

Understanding the Passage

6. According to the author, fishery scientists study the
   - ☐ a. effects of climate on evaporation.
   - ☐ b. breeding habits of sharks and whales.
   - ☐ c. location and growth of plant life.

7. Oceanographic research has discovered a relationship between
   - ☐ a. overfishing and fish weight.
   - ☐ b. shellfish reproduction and coral formations.
   - ☐ c. pleasure fishing and water salinities.

8. Marine scientists view the ocean as a
   - ☐ a. supplier of food.
   - ☐ b. potential source of fresh water.
   - ☐ c. logical place to begin climate control research.

9. An upset in maximum sustainable yields could result in
   - ☐ a. genetic changes in many species of fish.
   - ☐ b. the migration of fresh water fish to salt water.
   - ☐ c. the extinction of certain varieties of fish.

10. Once an equilibrium is established, it is
    - ☐ a. permanent.
    - ☐ b. temporary.
    - ☐ c. ineffective.

36

Remember, You're a Guest

If you're traveling on your own in Eastern Europe—Bulgaria, Czechoslovakia, Hungary, Poland, Romania, or the U.S.S.R., you should inform the American Embassy of your plans, including local addresses and dates of arrival and departure as stated in your visa and any later changes. United States embassies will need this information in case you encounter difficulties. Of course, if you're with an escorted tour, this task may be handled for you.

Since the United States is not represented in East Germany or Albania, there are no American officials there to help you. It's a good precaution to check in with an American Embassy or consulate in a nearby country to obtain the latest information on conditions and to leave a record of your travel plans.

Be sure you've met visa requirements before arriving and adhere strictly to the local customs and currency controls. Don't accept parcels or papers for delivery to third persons and don't attempt to travel on papers or passports issued by East European governments.

When entering a country, you will receive specific guidelines. Be sure you follow them. Don't buy items with dollars except in stores officially authorized to accept foreign money. Find these stores through local tourist offices.

Declare all currency you are carrying. When leaving, your statement of currency and valuables will be compared to your statement on entering. Keep receipts for all money transactions. Currency and travelers checks undeclared when entering a country may be taken from you when you leave.

Avoid black market dealings and currency dealings with private individuals. When driving, be very cautious. When taking pictures, don't shoot areas that could have military or strategic importance. When tempted to speak out on what may be considered the country's internal affairs, don't! Remember, you're a guest.

No matter how straight you play it, the U.S. State Department can't assure your safety. Unprovoked arrest or delay is rare, but not unknown. If it happens to you, ask for permission to notify the American Embassy. If you are turned down, keep asking—politely but persistently.

Some East European countries claim that naturalized United States citizens still keep their former nationality and are subject to local laws as citizens. If you feel that this may apply to you, check beforehand with the U.S. State Department to find out how you can formally end previous citizenship through the appropriate foreign embassy in Washington.

Recalling Facts

1. Which country is mentioned in the article?
   - ☐ a. France
   - ☐ b. Hungary
   - ☐ c. Turkey

2. American Embassies do not exist in
   - ☐ a. Russia.
   - ☐ b. Finland.
   - ☐ c. Albania.

3. A person who is denied permission to call an American Embassy should
   - ☐ a. be persistent.
   - ☐ b. call anyway.
   - ☐ c. give up.

4. One should avoid taking pictures of
   - ☐ a. public buildings.
   - ☐ b. military bases.
   - ☐ c. national monuments.

5. In East European countries, an unprovoked arrest or detainment is
   - ☐ a. rare.
   - ☐ b. common.
   - ☐ c. unknown.

Understanding the Passage

6. The author advises against
   - ☐ a. traveling in communist countries.
   - ☐ b. crossing borders with foreign goods.
   - ☐ c. retaining East European citizenship.

7. To develop the ideas in this article, the author uses
   - ☐ a. specific advice.
   - ☐ b. common-sense suggestions.
   - ☐ c. several actual incidents.

8. This article suggests that embassies
   - ☐ a. establish import quotas on gift items.
   - ☐ b. offer help to people traveling abroad.
   - ☐ c. issue passports in European countries.

9. The author expresses concern over the
   - ☐ a. lack of cooperation between countries.
   - ☐ b. poor hotels in Europe.
   - ☐ c. purchase of black market goods.

10. The author wrote this article for anyone who plans to
    - ☐ a. work for the American Embassy.
    - ☐ b. travel in Eastern Europe.
    - ☐ c. import goods from Asian countries.

37 A Dread Disease

Cancer is a word that stands for a large group of diseases that afflict man and animals. Cancer can arise in any organ or tissue of the body. Its main characteristic is an abnormal, seemingly unlimited growth of body cells. The resultant mass, or tumor, compresses, invades, and destroys adjacent normal tissues. Cancer cells can break off and leave the original mass. They can be carried by the blood or lymph to distant sites of the body. There they set up secondary growths further attacking and destroying the organs involved.

At the present time, at least 100 different types of cancer have been classified by their appearance under the microscope and by the site of the body in which they arise. Some of these grow very slowly and destroy neighboring tissue by limited spread. Others spread rapidly to distant sites. Most cancers occur in older people, but some forms are found most often in children.

Cancer cells do not necessarily appear strikingly different from normal cells. The body's normal repair of damaged tissue may for a limited time look quite "wild" in appearance under the microscope. On the other hand, a tumor that could be fatal if located in a vital area such as the brain, can seem benign, or innocent, in microscopic appearance. Again, although cancer tissues are generally characterized by a rapid growth rate, cell division and tissue growth in normal pregnancy may proceed at a greater pace. The most important difference is that the normal process stops when it has reached its end point, as in the healing of a cut or the completion of a pregnancy, whereas the cancerous process is uncontrolled.

The diseases grouped under cancer are second only to heart disease as killers of the people of the United States. This is true in other countries where infectious diseases and malnutrition also play relatively unimportant roles in causing deaths.

Of the more than 200 million people in the United States, during one year about 635,000 develop cancer and almost 280,000 die of it.

The effect of age is important in considering the rate of occurrence of cancer. The number of cancer deaths in the United States has increased steadily during the past 50 years. During this period, the percentage of older people has increased. The rate of occurrence of cancer in general and the rate of deaths for most cancers have not changed.

Recalling Facts

1. How many different types of cancer have been identified?
   - ☐ a. 25
   - ☐ b. 50
   - ☐ c. 100

2. Cancer types are classified according to their
   - ☐ a. rate of cell division.
   - ☐ b. appearance under the microscope.
   - ☐ c. chemical composition.

3. Cancer types are also classified by their
   - ☐ a. rate of spread.
   - ☐ b. resistance to drugs.
   - ☐ c. location in the body.

4. About how many Americans die from cancer annually?
   - ☐ a. 150,000
   - ☐ b. 250,000
   - ☐ c. 350,000

5. During the past fifty years, cancer deaths in the United States
   - ☐ a. have increased.
   - ☐ b. have decreased.
   - ☐ c. remained unchanged.

Understanding the Passage

6. According to the author, cancer cells
   - ☐ a. often look like healthy cells.
   - ☐ b. are usually marked by elongated bands of color.
   - ☐ c. are much smaller than normal cells.

7. The author states that
   - ☐ a. lung cancer has been linked with smoking.
   - ☐ b. cancer is not unusual in animals.
   - ☐ c. some forms of cancer are contagious.

8. From the information provided, the reader can assume that
   - ☐ a. cancer was unknown in ancient times.
   - ☐ b. cancer kills more people than heart disease.
   - ☐ c. no part of the body is immune to cancer.

9. The author implies that in the United States
   - ☐ a. infectious diseases contribute little to the death toll.
   - ☐ b. cancer is treated most commonly with radiation.
   - ☐ c. age has little bearing on incidence of cancer.

10. We can conclude that
    - ☐ a. microscopic examination of cancer tissue is sometimes deceptive.
    - ☐ b. cancer cells cease to grow after damaging one area.
    - ☐ c. cuts and scrapes often develop into cancerous tissues.

38 Shrinking and Swelling

In the office of a congressman from California a log cross section is displayed on the wall. Beautifully preserved and finished, it came from the base of a large red fir, the 1966 national Christmas tree, which was a perfectly formed forest giant grown in the congressman's home district.

This cross section is distinctive. It is free from the checks and the pie-shaped cracks that normally develop when a cross section is dried by conventional means.

The perfection of the congressman's wall display is due to a special chemical stabilization treatment. It is one application of knowledge gained from basic research aimed at finding ways to prevent wood from changing in dimension with variations in moisture content.

The chemical that has shown the greatest promise, and is now widely used in processing specialty wood products, is polyethylene glycol-1000, or PEG.

PEG is a white, waxlike chemical that resembles paraffin. It is nontoxic, dissolves readily in water, and will not discolor wood. When a piece of green wood is soaked for an appropriate period in a 30 to 50 percent water solution of PEG, the wood does not shrink appreciably when it is dried. Because there is little or no change in dimension, treated wood has less tendency to warp and is usually free of the checks and splits that so frequently develop in wood, especially thick stock, during the drying process. Wood that is treated and then dried swells very little when exposed again to high humidities.

PEG attacks the problem of changes in wood dimension where they start by bulking the microscopic, latticelike structure of the individual wood-fiber walls. Heavily treated wood is thus permanently restrained from shrinking, swelling, or warping regardless of atmospheric humidity.

Treatment with PEG permits efficient processing of green or partially dried wood, which is relatively inexpensive and plentiful. It is ideally suited to the manufacture of salad bowls, large serving trays, candlesticks, art carvings, gunstocks, and similar products that normally require thick pieces of the highest and most expensive grades of kiln-dried hardwoods.

Although wood is easily adaptable and widely used, its tendency to shrink and swell causes many problems. Almost everyone has been plagued by doors that swell and stick in hot, humid weather. Fine rifles lose their pinpoint accuracy due to a warped stock. Until PEG was discovered, scientists had been searching for solutions to such problems for more than forty years.

Recalling Facts

1. Expensive rifles sometimes lose their accuracy because of
   □ a. rusted barrels.
   □ b. warped stocks.
   □ c. coated sights.

2. The article mentions a congressman from the state of
   □ a. Virginia.
   □ b. Massachusetts.
   □ c. California.

3. The cross section of wood on the congressman's wall came from
   □ a. an oak.
   □ b. a red fir.
   □ c. a pine.

4. PEG is described as a
   □ a. swelling agent.
   □ b. stabilizer.
   □ c. moisturizing chemical.

5. What color is PEG?
   □ a. blue
   □ b. white
   □ c. yellow

Understanding the Passage

6. Molasses is to syrup as PEG is to
   □ a. wax.
   □ b. water.
   □ c. oil.

7. The author implies that PEG
   □ a. is always mixed with water before application.
   □ b. is usually used undiluted.
   □ c. must be applied in a well-ventilated room.

8. From the information provided, we can assume that untreated wood
   □ a. changes shape when it is subjected to high humidities.
   □ b. loses its resiliency when it is exposed to high temperatures.
   □ c. cracks when it is used in very wet places.

9. The article suggests that
   □ a. most hardware stores sell PEG.
   □ b. PEG is widely used in the construction of new homes.
   □ c. green wood is less expensive than aged wood.

10. The discovery of PEG
    □ a. occurred by accident.
    □ b. resulted from more than three decades of research.
    □ c. went unnoticed for many years.

39 Our Water Supply

America is in no immediate danger of "running out of water." However, water is certainly not inexhaustible. People in the arid West have always been aware that water is a precious commodity and must be conserved. In the humid East, an excess of water led to complacency until two factors created concern over our water supply. First, several periods of drought in recent years in the Northeast affected crop production and used up the surface and groundwater supplies. Secondly, attention was called to the rapid increases in the rates of pollution of these waters because of increased urban and industrial growth. As a result, people are becoming ● increasingly aware of the need for conserving both the quantity and quality of our nation's water supplies.

Many people don't realize that although it is a renewable resource, the water we use may not always be high quality. When used for municipal, industrial, or agricultural purposes, it is not destroyed, but generally finds its way back into our water supply. This used water now carries some waste material. These contaminated waters are often dumped into larger bodies of water or are disposed of on land. In the latter instance, evaporation concentrates some of the wastes on the soil surface. On the other ● hand, water moving through the soil will eventually carry some of the wastes down into the groundwater supplies. Eventually, all water evaporates and later returns to the earth as rain or snow in a relatively pure state.

Because of this never-ending cycle, there is just as much water in this country now as there has ever been. The amount, however, does not increase. Our rapid population growth and our rapid agricultural and industrial expansion have caused our water needs to soar. By withdrawing water from streams too rapidly and by depositing too much waste too ● quickly, we have in some instances upset the balance of nature's built-in renewal processes for conserving water. As a result, some of our streams and lakes have become "wet deserts." There is still plenty of water in them, but it is water so polluted that it supports almost no life at all.

We presently use almost 400 billion gallons of water a day. The estimated total freshwater supply is about 650 billion gallons per day. With our increasing needs, we must preserve the quality of every gallon of water so that it can be safely recycled.

Recalling Facts

1. Until recently, what section of the country felt complacent about existing water supplies?
   - ☐ a. the South
   - ☐ b. the West
   - ☐ c. the East

2. Water reserves today, compared with a hundred years ago, are
   - ☐ a. larger.
   - ☐ b. smaller.
   - ☐ c. the same.

3. How many billion gallons of water are used daily in this country?
   - ☐ a. 200
   - ☐ b. 300
   - ☐ c. 400

4. The Northeast was recently affected by drought and
   - ☐ a. water pollution.
   - ☐ b. livestock difficulties.
   - ☐ c. economic turmoil.

5. Nature's built-in renovation processes have been upset by
   - ☐ a. weather controls.
   - ☐ b. excessive use.
   - ☐ c. reservoir construction.

Understanding the Passage

6. This selection is about
   - ☐ a. water conservation programs in many American communities.
   - ☐ b. existing water supplies in various sections of the country.
   - ☐ c. America's use and misuse of water to meet today's needs.

7. The author feels that the danger of America's "running out of water" is
   - ☐ a. likely in the very near future.
   - ☐ b. greatly exaggerated by politicians.
   - ☐ c. not an immediate threat.

8. According to the author, water is not very polluted in
   - ☐ a. underground water supplies.
   - ☐ b. fast-moving streams and rivers.
   - ☐ c. rain and snow.

9. When the author says that lakes have become "wet deserts," she is
   - ☐ a. being sarcastic.
   - ☐ b. speaking literally.
   - ☐ c. using irony.

10. The author states that water
   - ☐ a. can be lost forever with misuse.
   - ☐ b. always evaporates from the earth's surface.
   - ☐ c. is not usually polluted by industry.

A Token of Peace

Many romantic legends have been inspired by Sacagawea, the Shoshone Indian woman who accompanied Lewis and Clark on much of their expedition of 1804-06.

One of President Jefferson's major purposes in commissioning Lewis and Clark to explore the newly acquired Louisiana Territory had been the establishing of friendly relations with Indian tribes between St. Louis and the Pacific Ocean. Indian chiefs were to be given Jefferson peace medals at these historic first contacts with white men.

In the winter of 1804, some 1,600 miles from their St. Louis starting point, Lewis and Clark arrived in the North Dakota country of the Mandan Indians, where they were befriended by the tribe and spent a peaceful winter. Living among the Mandans were a French Canadian fur trader, Touissaint Charbonneau, and his young Indian wife, Sacagawea. When the expedition left Mandan country, the couple went with it. Charbonneau was hired as an interpreter for $25 a month and Sacagawea carried her new-born baby on her back.

Sacagawea's main reason for accompanying the explorers was a longing to see her own Shoshone people again. Five years earlier, at the age of 12, she had been stolen by Crow Indians, taken far from her Rocky Mountain home, and sold as a slave to the Missouri River Mandans. In time, she had been sold to Charbonneau.

Sacagawea was of great value to the expedition in her role as peace envoy and intermediary with Indian tribes. Clark said of her, "Sacagawea reconciles all the Indians to our friendly intentions. A woman with a party of men is a token of peace."

Across the Missouri River, Lewis and Clark were faced with the snow-capped Rocky Mountains. Crossing them would be impossible without horses. Going on ahead, Lewis met a band of Shoshone Indians, and persuaded them to return with him to the expedition. With the tremendous advantage of Sacagawea's relationship, the explorers were able to barter for 29 Shoshone horses, and the journey continued.

Across the Rockies, the party built canoes and followed the Columbia River to the Pacific. The two explorers frequently praised Sacagawea's endurance and fortitude. She must have also been undemanding. Lewis wrote of her, "If she has enough to eat and a few trinkets to wear, I believe she would be perfectly content anywhere." Sacagawea was among those Indians honored with the prized Jefferson peace medal, evidence of the genuine fondness Lewis and Clark felt for her.

---

*Reading Time*_____ *Comprehension Score*_____ *Words per Minute*_____

Recalling Facts

1. The President who commissioned Lewis and Clark was
   - ☐ a. Jefferson.
   - ☐ b. Madison.
   - ☐ c. Jackson.

2. By the winter of 1804, Lewis and Clark had traveled more than
   - ☐ a. 500 miles.
   - ☐ b. 1,000 miles.
   - ☐ c. 1,500 miles.

3. Charbonneau was hired as an interpreter at a monthly salary of
   - ☐ a. $25.
   - ☐ b. $100.
   - ☐ c. $175.

4. Clark considered the presence of a woman in a group of men to be a
   - ☐ a. token of peace.
   - ☐ b. sign of good luck.
   - ☐ c. guarantee against attack.

5. The author mentions that Lewis and Clark crossed the
   - ☐ a. Mississippi River.
   - ☐ b. Missouri River.
   - ☐ c. Columbia River.

Understanding the Passage

6. Because of Sacagawea, the expedition was able to
   - ☐ a. trade items for horses.
   - ☐ b. find a lost Indian tribe.
   - ☐ c. build canoes.

7. Sacagawea is described as a
   - ☐ a. self-centered leader.
   - ☐ b. tireless person.
   - ☐ c. creative individual.

8. The author suggests that Sacagawea
   - ☐ a. is an important figure in American history.
   - ☐ b. was a personal friend of the President.
   - ☐ c. was not an Indian by birth.

9. The President wanted Lewis and Clark to give the Indians
   - ☐ a. parcels of land in the newly acquired territory.
   - ☐ b. small amounts of American money.
   - ☐ c. symbolic pieces of jewelry.

10. Sacagawea traveled with Lewis and Clark because she
   - ☐ a. was well paid for her work.
   - ☐ b. was needed as an interpreter.
   - ☐ c. wanted to visit her original tribe.

41　What Is Hotline?

As the nation has come to realize the critical proportions of its mental health needs, communities have sought new methods to aid individuals in distress. One of these methods is the telephone crisis intervention service, including those commonly referred to as Hotline. The Hotline approach depends basically upon voice communication via the telephone to aid an individual by allowing him the opportunity to interact with a trained listener. The number of Hotlines is steadily increasing, and many are designed with the adolescent in mind.

The Hotline approach works with young people for several reasons. First, Hotline provides an outlet for the adolescent through a caring individual, the listener who answers the phone. Most Hotlines are based upon the concept of creative listening, which includes a special sensitivity to the world of youth.

Second, Hotline poses a minimum of red tape to the caller. The service is immediate. As soon as a listener picks up the phone, the caller's communication with a caring individual has begun. The approach is based upon helping people with problems, rather than solving problems to which people are attached.

Young people who call Hotline have already taken a big step by admitting they are having difficulties that they can't solve alone. Each caller is exhibiting his desire to reach out.

A third reason the Hotline approach works is that the service respects the anonymity of the caller. In many situations, this act of reaching out would not occur if the caller had to reveal his identity. Most adolescents have fears of rejection, of ridicule, or of being judged. A call to Hotline has no strings attached. The listener is there to listen, to hear the caller out, and to assist the caller in finding possible ways to solve individual struggles and concerns.

The Hotline approach is aimed at reinforcing feelings of strength in an individual and to help him take positive strides in problem-solving. If the crisis experience is to yield dividends in terms of growth, the main focus must be upon the caller, his own resources, and his own needs.

The tasks of the listener, then, are to provoke inquiry, to aid the caller in examining what he is experiencing, and to help him reconsider or clarify his opinions about himself and his relationships with others. The goal is to oppose the tendency to rely upon external agents of change and to build greater self-confidence in solving problems.

Recalling Facts

1. Most Hotlines are based upon the concept of
   - ☐ a. skillful advice.
   - ☐ b. creative listening.
   - ☐ c. sensitive perceptions.

2. The function of Hotline is to
   - ☐ a. help people.
   - ☐ b. instruct patients.
   - ☐ c. solve problems.

3. The Hotline respects the caller's
   - ☐ a. anonymity.
   - ☐ b. religion.
   - ☐ c. illness.

4. Hotline directs callers to their own
   - ☐ a. resources.
   - ☐ b. parents.
   - ☐ c. clergymen.

5. The task of the listener is to provoke
   - ☐ a. complacency.
   - ☐ b. anger.
   - ☐ c. inquiry.

Understanding the Passage

6. After speaking with Hotline, a person should
   - ☐ a. know where to turn with his problems.
   - ☐ b. have greater confidence in himself.
   - ☐ c. consider visiting a Hotline officer in person.

7. The Hotline was set up originally as a
   - ☐ a. guidance counseling service in public schools.
   - ☐ b. telephone crisis service.
   - ☐ c. network of regional mental health clinics.

8. Hotline services are often used by
   - ☐ a. drug addicts.
   - ☐ b. adolescents.
   - ☐ c. depressive housewives.

9. The author implies that the Hotline is
   - ☐ a. a free public service.
   - ☐ b. sponsored by local businesspeople.
   - ☐ c. affiliated with the American Medical Association.

10. We can conclude that
   - ☐ a. most callers feel inadequate.
   - ☐ b. a person uses the Hotline service only once.
   - ☐ c. Hotline listeners are trained psychologists.

National wildlife refuges are lands for people as well as wildlife.

Blackwater National Wildlife Refuge is located on Maryland's Eastern Shore, less than two hours from the Washington-Baltimore metropolitan area. It is one of the more people-oriented of the Fish and Wildlife Service's 350 refuges. The 11,627-acre area offers refreshing relief from the city's atmosphere. Fields, woods, and marshes replace asphalt, concrete, and steel. The honkings of wild geese replace the din of city traffic.

Hundreds of people visit the refuge on fall weekends when migratory waterfowl are at peak abundance. Seasonal changes of habitat and wildlife make the refuge inviting during all seasons.

Newcomers seek information at the visitor center, where exhibits indicate the wildlife species common to the refuge. Films and slide programs are often shown to provide further familiarization.

By arriving at the right moment, one can watch a live wildlife performance through large windows at the rear of the center. Geese come in by the hundreds from feeding flights to nearby fields. With incessant honking, they tumble out of the sky, spilling the air from their wings and gracefully gliding down upon the water of the impoundment constructed for them.

From the center, visitors are directed to the wildlife drive that passes through woods and fields, diked ponds and marshes. Great blue herons stalk the shallow waters, and deer graze at the far reaches of a bordering field, ready to flee into the woods at the first sight of danger. In warmer months, turtles lazily sun themselves on fallen logs, and egrets and shore birds wade along the water's edge.

A picnic area and observation tower are located off a side road near the entrance to the wildlife drive. The tower, an old converted fire tower, overlooks a vast area of river and marsh and offers a good panorama of the refuge. The structure is also a suitable place from which to glimpse the endangered Southern bald eagle that uses the small tree islands and wooded edges of the marsh as nesting and roosting sites. Sunlight glances off his bold white head as he soars high above the river, then swoops to catch a fish in the dark waters.

A trail for walkers winds through a mixed pine-hardwood forest, managed habitat of the endangered Delmarva Peninsula fox squirrel, or "big gray" as he is called locally. Deer, songbirds, and the common gray squirrel are also present.

*Reading Time*_____   *Comprehension Score*_____   *Words per Minute*_____

Recalling Facts

1. The Blackwater National Wildlife Refuge is located in
   - ☐ a. Kentucky.
   - ☐ b. Maryland.
   - ☐ c. Virginia.

2. The Fish and Wildlife Service operates more than
   - ☐ a. 300 refuges.
   - ☐ b. 700 refuges.
   - ☐ c. 1,200 refuges.

3. The observation tower was once a
   - ☐ a. fire tower.
   - ☐ b. television tower.
   - ☐ c. water tower.

4. "Big gray" is the nickname for
   - ☐ a. a bear.
   - ☐ b. an eagle.
   - ☐ c. a squirrel.

5. In the refuge, a visitor can see
   - ☐ a. grazing bison.
   - ☐ b. live crocodiles.
   - ☐ c. blue herons.

Understanding the Passage

6. The author implies that most visitors come during the
   - ☐ a. fall.
   - ☐ b. spring.
   - ☐ c. summer.

7. The Southern bald eagle likes to build its nests
   - ☐ a. on steep cliffs.
   - ☐ b. near lakes and rivers.
   - ☐ c. in rocky fields.

8. Exhibits in the visitors' center
   - ☐ a. show exotic tropical birds in their natural habitats.
   - ☐ b. portray extinct birds and wildlife.
   - ☐ c. offer a view of animal life in the refuge itself.

9. During the warm summer months,
   - ☐ a. turtles like to sun themselves.
   - ☐ b. geese leave the refuge to fly north.
   - ☐ c. the visitors' center offers evening tours to the public.

10. We can conclude that
   - ☐ a. the Blackwater National Wildlife Refuge is closed during the winter months.
   - ☐ b. most wildlife refuges offer discount rates to large touring groups.
   - ☐ c. wild birds and animals are attracted to the Blackwater National Refuge.

43

The Surrender at Yorktown

The surrender of the British army at Yorktown on October 19, 1781, marked the close of the American Revolution. It ended almost seven years of war. While the treaty of peace was not signed until later, the victory at Yorktown was the decisive event in the struggle to make the United States an independent nation.

In 1781, the British had practically abandoned efforts to reconquer the northern states. But they still had hopes of regaining the South. That spring, Lieutenant General Earl Cornwallis marched into Virginia from North Carolina. He believed that if Virginia could be subdued, the states to the south would readily return to British allegiance.

The Marquis de Lafayette, operating in Virginia with a small American force, was unable to meet Cornwallis in open battle. The British army marched up and down the state almost at will, but failed to break the resistance of the people. Cornwallis was directed to fortify a naval base in the lower Chesapeake.

Cornwallis chose Yorktown for the base and transferred his army there early in August. He began fortifying the town and Gloucester Point across the river. Meanwhile, a French fleet under Count de Grasse was moving up for combined operations with the allied French and American armies. Count de Grasse blockaded the mouth of Chesapeake Bay, cutting off Cornwallis from help by sea. Washington then moved his forces toward Virginia to attack by land. These forces included part of the main American army operating on the Hudson and the French army under Count de Rochambeau.

While de Grasse maintained a blockade by sea, the combined armies gathered at Williamsburg. On September 28th, they marched down the peninsula and laid siege to Yorktown, with its British garrison of 7,500. Cornwallis almost immediately abandoned his outer line and retired within the town. During the night of October 6, the allied armies opened entrenchments and a few days later began a heavy bombardment of the British position. Their fire soon subdued Cornwallis, and the allies were able to close in at shorter range. Two outlying British forts were stormed. The British army was then in an extremely desperate position. Cornwallis made an attempt to escape by way of Gloucester, but his boats were scattered by a storm. On the morning of October 17, he sent out a flag of truce and asked Washington for a discussion of terms of surrender.

*Reading Time*_____ *Comprehension Score*_____ *Words per Minute*_____

Recalling Facts

1. The British army surrendered at Yorktown in the early
   - ☐ a. 1770s.
   - ☐ b. 1780s.
   - ☐ c. 1790s.

2. The American Revolution lasted almost
   - ☐ a. seven years.
   - ☐ b. nine years.
   - ☐ c. eleven years.

3. Cornwallis felt that the most important state to conquer in the South was
   - ☐ a. Kentucky.
   - ☐ b. Georgia.
   - ☐ c. Virginia.

4. American forces were aided by the
   - ☐ a. Germans.
   - ☐ b. French.
   - ☐ c. Canadians.

5. Yorktown's British garrison comprised
   - ☐ a. 2,500 men.
   - ☐ b. 5,500 men.
   - ☐ c. 7,500 men.

Understanding the Passage

6. The author implies that Count de Grasse was
   - ☐ a. a naval commander.
   - ☐ b. a personal friend of Washington.
   - ☐ c. an expert in land strategy.

7. Williamsburg is mentioned as
   - ☐ a. the city of a great American defeat.
   - ☐ b. a British base of operations.
   - ☐ c. a meeting place of allied forces.

8. The surrender of Cornwallis can be viewed as a
   - ☐ a. bloody encounter.
   - ☐ b. diplomatic settlement.
   - ☐ c. fateful accident.

9. The author states that Cornwallis was
   - ☐ a. defeated because of poor planning.
   - ☐ b. unable to escape because of bad weather.
   - ☐ c. an expert naval officer.

10. We can conclude that the American victory
    - ☐ a. ended the British occupation of America.
    - ☐ b. divided the country into halves.
    - ☐ c. was the only battle lost by the British.

44

Water for Industry

Industrial uses of water are commonly divided into four categories: cooling water, process water, boiler feedwater, and sanitary and service water. Cooling water is water used only for cooling without coming into contact with the product or material being processed. Process water is water that comes into contact with material being processed. Boiler feedwater is water converted to steam. Sanitary and service water is that supplied for the personal use of the employees, for cleaning plants and equipment, and for the operation of valves and other apparatus.

About 90 percent of the water withdrawn by industry is used for cooling. Fuel-electric power plants use more cooling water than all other kinds of plants combined. One might suppose that the greatest amount of water used in the fuel-electric power production is used for boiler feedwater, but such use is dwarfed by the water needed for cooling condensers. Cooling water is also used to condense many products of oil refineries and chemical plants and to protect industrial equipment from excessive heat. A blast furnace in a steel plant may use as much as 35 million gallons of water per day.

Most manufacturing plants use process water at some point in the course of their operations. In some plants the material being processed is in contact with water at almost every step in its conversion to the finished product. For example, in the production of pulp and paper, water is used for removing bark from pulp wood, moving the ground wood and pulp from one process to another, cooking the wood chips, and washing the pulp. The cooling liquors are made up of various chemicals, such as sodium sulfite and sodium hydroxide, which are dissolved in water. Water also serves as a solvent for chemicals in many other chemical processes; and the food industry uses large quantities of water for cleaning, cooking, and canning vegetables and meats.

Another important use of water by industry is for disposal of its waste products. At one time, streamflows were adequate to dilute, dissolve, or carry away these wastes. However, some rivers in the United States are being progressively depleted by use and overloaded with wastes. This pollution not only upsets the delicate natural balance among plants, insects, and fish, but also poses problems of water quality for the people and industries downstream. Many communities have begun conservation and clean-up programs in order to preserve rivers and waterways, and to increase their productivity.

Recalling Facts

1. Water that is converted to steam is called
   - ☐ a. cooling water.
   - ☐ b. process water.
   - ☐ c. boiler feedwater.

2. Water used by industry to operate valves is called
   - ☐ a. service water.
   - ☐ b. process water.
   - ☐ c. cooling water.

3. How much water is used by industry for cooling?
   - ☐ a. 30 percent
   - ☐ b. 60 percent
   - ☐ c. 90 percent

4. The greatest amount of cooling water is used in
   - ☐ a. iron smelting foundries.
   - ☐ b. electric power plants.
   - ☐ c. canning factories.

5. How much water does a blast furnace require daily?
   - ☐ a. fifteen million gallons
   - ☐ b. twenty-five million gallons
   - ☐ c. thirty-five million gallons

Understanding the Passage

6. Paper is mentioned as an example of an industry that
   - ☐ a. pollutes streams and rivers.
   - ☐ b. uses water in every step of production.
   - ☐ c. uses very little water.

7. The author points out that some chemicals
   - ☐ a. dissolve in water.
   - ☐ b. make water toxic.
   - ☐ c. increase the flow of water.

8. From the article, the reader can assume that
   - ☐ a. large amounts of water are used in mining coal.
   - ☐ b. condensers can overheat without water.
   - ☐ c. special water rates are given to large industries.

9. The most important use of industrial water is for
   - ☐ a. servicing.
   - ☐ b. processing.
   - ☐ c. protecting equipment.

10. The author shows concern about the
    - ☐ a. depletion and pollution of rivers.
    - ☐ b. danger of pressurized water.
    - ☐ c. use of chemicals in industry.

From the time of George Washington, our Presidents have been interested in the Potomac. But it wasn't until February 1965 that a President took a positive stand on the river and its future.

In a "Message on the Natural Beauty of Our Country," President Lyndon B. Johnson stated that the Potomac should become a model of both conservation and beauty for the nation. The President directed the Secretary of the Interior to develop a plan to "clean up the river and keep it clean," to protect the natural beauty of the river and its basin, and to assure a supply of water from the river and other sources to meet municipal needs for the decades ahead. The plan also had to provide adequate flood control and to give maximum recreational opportunities to people who live along the river and its tributaries and to those who visit the river basin.

Judging from the *Potomac Interim Report to the President*, published a year later in January 1966, the Interdepartmental Task Force, which was established to develop the plan, decided to first draw up a master plan for recreation. The plan provided for recreation and natural beauty by requiring high levels of water quality and public control of access to the river and its major tributaries, through easement or ownership of the flood plains and the shoreline.

For the Potomac to become the model conservation and recreation success which the President expected, the quality of the water in the river had to improve significantly. There had to be more rigid limitations on the amounts of organic pollutants entering this river and sediment had to be kept out of the Potomac by effective erosion control measures.

The model plan for the Potomac is abundantly clear. The plan is an expression of demand—primarily a demand for the water-based recreation which has already been mentioned.

And this recreation requirement stems principally from the pressing needs of the Washington, D.C., region where two-thirds of the basin's 3.5 million people live without many satisfactory opportunities for outdoor recreation. While offending accuracy somewhat—for the sake of simplicity—one can fairly say that the model plan represents but another chapter in a lengthy catalog of demands that Washington, D.C. and its suburbs have placed on the water and the land resources of the far-flung Potomac Basin. It is hoped that the issue of environmental cleanliness in and around the Potomac Basin will not be forgotten.

Recalling Facts

1. The first President to take a positive stand on the Potomac River issue was
   - ☐ a. Truman.
   - ☐ b. Kennedy.
   - ☐ c. Johnson.

2. The project of cleaning the Potomac River was assigned to the Department of
   - ☐ a. the Interior.
   - ☐ b. Agriculture.
   - ☐ c. State.

3. The first master plan for the Potomac was concerned with
   - ☐ a. irrigation.
   - ☐ b. municipal water.
   - ☐ c. recreation.

4. Over the years, sediment accumulated in the river because of
   - ☐ a. erosion.
   - ☐ b. chemical dumping.
   - ☐ c. residential misuse.

5. About how many people live in the Potomac River basin?
   - ☐ a. 2 million
   - ☐ b. 3.5 million
   - ☐ c. 5 million

Understanding the Passage

6. The article implies that the Potomac River
   - ☐ a. was more polluted than the Mississippi River.
   - ☐ b. flows by Washington, D.C.
   - ☐ c. supplies drinking water to several communities.

7. Recreational facilities along the Potomac will
   - ☐ a. include several large tennis courts.
   - ☐ b. not allow hunting or swimming.
   - ☐ c. be open to out-of-state tourists.

8. The author implies that the Potomac River
   - ☐ a. has threatened lowland areas with flooding.
   - ☐ b. will furnish hydroelectric power to a large area.
   - ☐ c. was cut into the landscape by the retreating ice sheet.

9. The *Potomac Interim Report to the President*
   - ☐ a. was drawn up under the supervision of the Vice President.
   - ☐ b. required about twelve months of research to complete.
   - ☐ c. amounted to three large volumes of material.

10. We can conclude that
    - ☐ a. water pollution can be reversible.
    - ☐ b. polluted water can be used for agricultural purposes.
    - ☐ c. the Potomac River basin has become a wildlife refuge.

46 Fearless Globetrotters

Birds such as the bobwhite, quail, and cardinal never fly more than ten miles from the nests where they were hatched. But arctic terns are true globetrotters. These birds nest in Greenland and the northern part of North America. A few are found as far south as Massachusetts. As soon as the young are grown, those from eastern North America cross the Atlantic Ocean to Europe. A few months later, they can be found in the Antarctic regions, 11,000 miles from their nesting grounds. They fly at least 25,000 miles each year when migrating.

Most North American birds, however, spend winters in southern United States and Central and South America. Coastal marshes along the Gulf of Mexico and along the South Atlantic coast of the United States serve as the winter home for hundreds of thousands of ducks.

Many dangers are faced by migrating birds during their long journeys. Aerial objects such as television or radio towers are responsible for the deaths of thousands each year. Airport towers and planes landing and taking off at airports are also dangerous for birds flying at night because some are drawn to the light during foggy weather.

The famous Washington Monument in our nation's capital, which is lighted by large searchlights, kills many birds, especially when there are gusty winds and a low cloud cover. The Statue of Liberty, when the torch is lighted, causes massive destruction of birds.

Storms also kill many birds, particularly the smaller ones. Inland hailstorms kill great numbers. Those crossing large stretches of water are sometimes forced down and drown. But birds like the sandpiper, plover, and tern are able to make long overseas flights. For example, the golden plover, traveling the Atlantic oceanic route from Nova Scotia to South America, covers the entire distance of 2,400 miles without stopping. Although much fat is lost, the bird seems little worse for wear as a result of its journey.

Bird migration had its start such a long time ago that it is only possible to guess at how it all began. Some aspects of migration, particularly routes of travel and time of year, have been worked out largely through banding efforts and sightings from planes, radar, and miniature radio transmitters. Interested observers and laboratory experiments have also contributed to the growing knowledge. But much of bird migration is still a mystery for future generations of scientists and amateur naturalists to explore.

*Reading Time*_____ *Comprehension Score*_____ *Words per Minute*_____   105

Recalling Facts

1. A bird that never flies more than ten miles from its nest is the
   - ☐ a. robin.
   - ☐ b. quail.
   - ☐ c. sparrow.

2. Arctic terns annually migrate
   - ☐ a. 5,000 miles.
   - ☐ b. 15,000 miles.
   - ☐ c. 25,000 miles.

3. The author mentions that birds are attracted to
   - ☐ a. planes.
   - ☐ b. windows.
   - ☐ c. lights.

4. Arctic terns seldom nest any further south than
   - ☐ a. Michigan.
   - ☐ b. Massachusetts.
   - ☐ c. Virginia.

5. Ducks spend the winter
   - ☐ a. around the Great Lakes.
   - ☐ b. in the New England states.
   - ☐ c. along the South Atlantic coast.

Understanding the Passage

6. Plovers and terns are described as
   - ☐ a. large, powerful fighters.
   - ☐ b. small insect eaters.
   - ☐ c. tireless fliers.

7. The Washington Monument is mentioned as
   - ☐ a. one of the most popular tourist attractions in the U.S.
   - ☐ b. a favorite nesting place for migrating birds.
   - ☐ c. a deathtrap for birds.

8. The author implies that
   - ☐ a. most birds do not migrate more than 500 miles.
   - ☐ b. birds fear lightning storms more than anything else.
   - ☐ c. some birds can fly farther than others.

9. This article is based on
   - ☐ a. scientific observations.
   - ☐ b. biased opinions.
   - ☐ c. generalized concepts.

10. We can assume that
    - ☐ a. birds are excellent swimmers.
    - ☐ b. most birds migrate without stopping.
    - ☐ c. the study of bird migration is in its infancy.

For the Cause of Liberty

The American colonies might not have had the needed strength to implement the Declaration of Independence without the aid of France. Certainly the leaders of the rebelling colonists knew the importance of French aid and began to seek such help soon after the outbreak of the American Revolution. In the autumn of 1775, the Continental Congress appointed a secret committee of foreign correspondents. Early the next year the committee sent an agent to France to seek the aid of that nation in the struggle against Great Britain. Silas Deane was selected for the task. Within a few months after his arrival in France, Deane, secretly aided by the French government, obtained and sent to America clothing and arms in large quantities. Deane also obtained for America all aid short of actual military support until 1778.

In addition, many French soldiers, as individuals, offered their assistance to the American cause. One of the most famous of these was the Marquis de Lafayette, who left his wife, fortune, and high social position to serve the cause of liberty. Popular with the American officers and a favorite of General Washington, the young Marquis was an able general. He played an important part in the defeat of Cornwallis in the final campaign of the Revolution.

Congress, in September of 1776, had appointed Benjamin Franklin and Arthur Lee as commissioners to France to work with Deane in securing a treaty of alliance. For over a year the commission labored at its task. Then came the news of the American triumph at Saratoga. When word of this important victory reached the French king, he promptly sent word to the commissioners that he would sign a treaty such as had been proposed. He also said that France would openly aid America with a fleet, troops, and money.

The Americans were greatly encouraged by the French alliance. Until then, the English had had the great advantage of supremacy at sea. Thenceforth, the French fleet forced England, in resisting French attacks, to use many ships that could otherwise have been used in transporting troops and supplies to America. The French Army greatly increased the numbers of American land forces. The final victory over the British at Yorktown was made possible by the French fleet and Army. Thus, throughout the long struggle of the Revolution, the sympathy and help of the French people were an invaluable aid to the American cause.

Recalling Facts

1. Silas Deane was an American ambassador to
   - ☐ a. England.
   - ☐ b. France.
   - ☐ c. Spain.

2. The Marquis de Lafayette became
   - ☐ a. a general.
   - ☐ b. a diplomat.
   - ☐ c. an aide to Washington.

3. The French king delayed the signing of the treaty of alliance for over a
   - ☐ a. week.
   - ☐ b. month.
   - ☐ c. year.

4. The final victory over the British occurred at
   - ☐ a. Saratoga.
   - ☐ b. Jamestown.
   - ☐ c. Yorktown.

5. Benjamin Franklin is mentioned as
   - ☐ a. a signer of the Declaration of Independence.
   - ☐ b. a commissioner to France.
   - ☐ c. an early presidential candidate.

Understanding the Passage

6. According to the author, the Marquis de Lafayette was
   - ☐ a. wealthy.
   - ☐ b. educated.
   - ☐ c. elderly.

7. The author implies that Cornwallis was a
   - ☐ a. traitor to the American cause.
   - ☐ b. noted British leader.
   - ☐ c. French aristocrat.

8. The French did not support the American colonies until
   - ☐ a. the British lost a decisive battle.
   - ☐ b. a president had been elected.
   - ☐ c. the French king was guaranteed payment in gold.

9. The French alliance helped the American colonies to establish
   - ☐ a. a strong fighting force at sea.
   - ☐ b. free trade with European nations.
   - ☐ c. French dominance in North America.

10. We can conclude that
    - ☐ a. French soldiers were paid well for their work.
    - ☐ b. without French aid, America may have lost the war.
    - ☐ c. France has always been America's closest ally.

Exploratory fishing is a scientific approach to the location of new fishery resources. Science has been able to predict with great accuracy the location of shrimp grounds. The main domestic fishing for shrimp has been conducted along the southern Atlantic and Gulf coasts of the United States.

In the Atlantic Ocean, exploratory vessels, using knowledge of the life history of shrimp and the type of environment that they prefer, located an extremely valuable shrimp ground off the Guianas of South America. A large fleet of United States shrimp trawlers is now fishing this area.

Once caught, how can fish and shellfish be best preserved and utilized? This is the work of fishery food science and technology, a branch of science as complex as the study of the ocean. Research is developing new techniques to bring the harvest of the sea and of fresh waters to the consumer in many new forms.

Many small marine animals, which are among the most abundant renewable resources in the ocean, are not utilized to full capacity or are not used at all. The very large and prolific group of herring and herringlike fishes now provides about one-third of the world's fishery catch. Increased catches of this group and other small schooling fishes are possible in many places.

Most of the herring and herringlike fishes are processed into fishmeal and oil. The meal is a high protein ingredient which is widely used in the feeding of poultry and livestock. The oil, which is a byproduct obtained during the preparation of the fishmeal, goes principally into margarine and paints.

Fishery scientists here and abroad are interested in using small fish more efficiently as direct food for humans. A high-protein edible meal, known as fish protein concentrate (FPC), has great potential for providing underfed and undernourished people with much-needed animal protein.

The staff of a laboratory in Maryland has developed a chemical method for extracting oil and water from fish, leaving a dry, powdery, protein-rich substance that can be produced for less than a dollar a pound. Only a fraction of a pound of this FPC is necessary daily to provide a person with the animal protein needed to balance a plant protein diet. A pilot plant is being planned on our Pacific coast to produce FPC commercially. The raw material for this protein food will be Pacific hake, which is abundant and virtually unutilized.

*Reading Time*_____ *Comprehension Score*_____ *Words per Minute*_____   109

Recalling Facts

1. Valuable shrimp grounds have been located recently
   - ☐ a. off the coast of Cuba.
   - ☐ b. at the mouth of the Mississippi River.
   - ☐ c. off the coast of South America.

2. Herring oil is used in the manufacture of
   - ☐ a. mayonnaise.
   - ☐ b. margarine.
   - ☐ c. yogurt.

3. Fishmeal is used as feed for
   - ☐ a. dogs.
   - ☐ b. chickens.
   - ☐ c. hamsters.

4. FPC is a good source of
   - ☐ a. minerals.
   - ☐ b. carbohydrates.
   - ☐ c. protein.

5. Pacific hake is a type of
   - ☐ a. seaweed.
   - ☐ b. shellfish.
   - ☐ c. fish.

Understanding the Passage

6. The author implies that
   - ☐ a. tuna is becoming extinct.
   - ☐ b. shrimp locations can be predicted.
   - ☐ c. shellfish is sometimes taken from polluted waters.

7. The reader can assume that
   - ☐ a. a form of herring is part of American diets.
   - ☐ b. swordfish often contains dangerous levels of mercury.
   - ☐ c. shrimp is the most expensive seafood in eastern restaurants.

8. The article implies that
   - ☐ a. the manufacture of FPC is a fairly simple process.
   - ☐ b. some primitive peoples are allergic to milk.
   - ☐ c. many countries intrude into American fishing grounds.

9. A vegetarian may be able to
   - ☐ a. maintain good health by eating only hake.
   - ☐ b. get enough protein by eating FPC.
   - ☐ c. catch his own marine animals.

10. According to the article,
   - ☐ a. small fish reproduce rapidly.
   - ☐ b. the United States has banned whaling.
   - ☐ c. water pollution has endangered many species of fish.

A Symbol of the Free Spirit

We do not know the tribe of men that first used the horse. Scientists tell us our ancestors were eating horses long before they domesticated them. Historians claim that horses were harnessed before they were ridden.

The horse-drawn chariot dates back to 2000 B.C. in actual records, and there is evidence it had been in use for a thousand years before that.

We also know the modern horse evolved from the dog-sized Eohippus. Its ancestors found their ecological niche on the open grasslands. There they developed the specializations that gave them the speed to outrun their predators and survive.

Fossil remains of the horse and all of its ancestors are common throughout much of North America. For many years, paleontologists believed that the horse first developed here, but later finds on the Euro-Asian continent have now raised questions about this theory. Whatever its origins, we do know that the horse either migrated to or from the Western Hemisphere and eventually became extinct in the New World.

Spanish conquistadors brought the horse back to the Western Hemisphere. In 1519 Cortés landed his troops and his herds of horses at the site of present-day Vera Cruz, Mexico. Coronado's expedition in 1540–41 took the horse to the plains of Kansas. Through the years, some of these Spanish horses escaped or were abandoned, and these became the nucleus of the first wild horse herds in North America.

Between 1519, when Cortés landed in Mexico, and 1803, when Lewis and Clark made their expedition into the West, was a period of 284 years. In the course of history, this is a considerable span of years—ample time to allow the great increase in the number of wild horses that had taken place by the time the pioneers began moving westward during our national expansion.

Western grasslands provided an ideal habitat for the horse and a population explosion occurred. A few horses were captured by the Indians, but this had no significant impact on the wild horse population. By the time English-speaking settlers reached the West, the wild bands were firmly established, and it appeared they had always been a part of the Western scene.

The image of the wild horse running free on the open plains has captured the mind and imagination of modern America and has become a symbol of the free spirit.

Recalling Facts

1. Scientists know that the horse-drawn chariot dates back to
   - ☐ a. A.D. 500.
   - ☐ b. 1000 B.C.
   - ☐ c. 2000 B.C.

2. The modern horse evolved from an animal about the size of
   - ☐ a. a dog.
   - ☐ b. an elephant.
   - ☐ c. a zebra.

3. The horse's ancestors found their ecological niche
   - ☐ a. on plains.
   - ☐ b. in forests.
   - ☐ c. near deserts.

4. For many years, scientists thought that the horse evolved in
   - ☐ a. Africa.
   - ☐ b. North America.
   - ☐ c. South America.

5. Cortés brought herds of horses to Mexico during the early
   - ☐ a. 1400s.
   - ☐ b. 1500s.
   - ☐ c. 1600s.

Understanding the Passage

6. The West provided an ideal habitat for horses because
   - ☐ a. the weather was temperate.
   - ☐ b. the area was mostly grasslands.
   - ☐ c. larger predatory animals had not reached the West.

7. Horses defended themselves against attack by
   - ☐ a. kicking their hoofs.
   - ☐ b. using their sharp teeth.
   - ☐ c. fleeing at great speed.

8. When Coronado explored the West, he
   - ☐ a. found many herds of wild horses.
   - ☐ b. captured many wild horses to take home with him.
   - ☐ c. lost a number of horses that later became wild.

9. The author ends the article on a tone of
   - ☐ a. sorrow.
   - ☐ b. sympathy.
   - ☐ c. nostalgia.

10. The author implies that American Indians
    - ☐ a. nearly depleted the wild horse population.
    - ☐ b. captured some wild horses for their own use.
    - ☐ c. brought most of their horses from Mexico.

50 The Tireless John Ross

In October of 1828, a blue-eyed, fair-skinned man stood before the General Council of the Cherokee Indian tribe. He raised his right hand and pledged, "I do solemnly swear that I will faithfully execute the office of Principal Chief of the Cherokee Nation and will, to the best of my ability, preserve, protect, and defend the Constitution of the Cherokee Nation."

John Ross, the man who took the oath of office so much like that of United States presidents, had many white relatives. But his Scottish immigrant father had brought John up as an Indian among Indians. John Ross thought of himself as a Cherokee, grew up to marry a Cherokee girl, and was to devote his life to leadership of the people he loved.

By the time Ross took his oath as Principal Chief of the new Cherokee government, the tribe had gone far toward civilization. They were accomplished farmers, cattlemen, and weavers. They had built roads, schools, and churches. Through the invention of a Cherokee alphabet, they were largely literate. In 1826, the Cherokee Nation formed a government patterned after that of the United States, its capital at New Echota, Georgia.

John Ross was the logical choice as Principal Chief, for he had been a tribal leader since 1813, when he had fought under General Jackson. As president of the Cherokee National Committee from 1819 to 1826, he had promoted the education and mechanical training of the Indians and had worked in development of the new government.

But the Cherokees' golden age was to be a brief one, for as early as 1802 the federal government had promised the state of Georgia that Indians would be removed from their lands. In 1822, the House of Representatives voted to take away Cherokee land titles. The Cherokee Council responded by voting to make no more treaties with the United States. Neither persuasion, threats, nor the bribery attempts of two commissioners from Washington could change Cherokee resistance.

Since Georgia maintained that the Indians were only tenants on their lands, the legislature ruthlessly stripped the Cherokees of all their civil rights. When gold was discovered on tribal lands, Cherokee fate was sealed. Answering demands of the Georgia legislature, the U.S. Congress appropriated $50,000 for removal of the tribe.

John Ross worked tirelessly, but unsuccessfully, in defending the right of Cherokees to their ancestral lands.

Recalling Facts

1. John Ross was famous as an Indian
   - ☐ a. medicine man.
   - ☐ b. chief.
   - ☐ c. teacher.

2. The father of John Ross was
   - ☐ a. Scottish.
   - ☐ b. Irish.
   - ☐ c. English.

3. John Ross married
   - ☐ a. an Iroquois.
   - ☐ b. a Cherokee.
   - ☐ c. a white girl.

4. The capital of the Cherokee Nation was located in
   - ☐ a. Alabama.
   - ☐ b. New Mexico.
   - ☐ c. Georgia.

5. The Cherokees were removed from their land at a cost of
   - ☐ a. $50,000.
   - ☐ b. $100,000.
   - ☐ c. $200,000.

Understanding the Passage

6. John Ross felt that the Indians were entitled to their land because they
   - ☐ a. bought it legally from the United States government.
   - ☐ b. won it fairly in a war settlement.
   - ☐ c. inherited it from their forefathers.

7. At the time that Ross became an important Indian figure, the
   - ☐ a. Cherokee Nation was living in fear of the white man.
   - ☐ b. Cherokees were an advanced people.
   - ☐ c. Cherokees were fighting among themselves.

8. John Ross gained military experience
   - ☐ a. fighting against the U.S. Army.
   - ☐ b. helping other tribes in the French and Indian War.
   - ☐ c. marching with American generals during the early 1800s.

9. The final defeat of the Cherokees came with the
   - ☐ a. discovery of gold on their land.
   - ☐ b. establishment of Indian reservations in the West.
   - ☐ c. death of John Ross.

10. We can conclude that
    - ☐ a. the Cherokees were victimized by state and federal governments.
    - ☐ b. John Ross prevented the government from taking Indian lands.
    - ☐ c. John Ross helped to develop the first Cherokee alphabet.

Answer Key

Progress Graph

Pacing Graph

Answer Key

	1.	2.	3.	4.	5.	6.	7.	8.	9.	10.
1	a	b	c	a	c	a	a	b	a	c
2	b	a	c	c	b	c	c	c	b	a
3	b	c	c	b	b	a	b	c	c	c
4	c	c	b	b	c	a	c	b	b	a
5	c	c	b	b	a	a	a	c	b	c
6	b	c	a	c	b	c	c	a	c	c
7	c	a	c	b	a	b	a	b	c	a
8	a	a	a	c	b	b	c	c	a	c
9	c	a	c	c	a	b	a	b	c	a
10	c	a	b	a	c	c	a	c	b	b
11	a	b	a	c	a	c	b	a	b	c
12	b	c	a	c	c	c	b	a	a	c
13	c	a	b	b	a	b	b	b	c	b
14	c	c	c	c	c	a	c	c	a	a
15	b	c	b	b	c	a	b	a	b	a
16	b	c	b	c	c	c	c	c	b	a
17	c	c	b	a	c	c	a	b	a	b
18	c	b	c	a	c	b	c	b	b	a
19	c	b	a	b	a	c	a	b	a	b
20	a	a	b	c	a	c	a	a	c	c
21	b	b	a	b	b	b	a	c	b	a
22	a	c	a	c	a	c	b	b	c	b
23	b	c	c	a	c	c	c	b	a	c
24	b	a	c	b	c	c	a	c	a	a
25	b	c	b	b	a	b	a	b	c	b

26	1. b	2. c	3. c	4. a	5. a	6. c	7. b	8. a	9. c	10. c
27	1. c	2. c	3. c	4. c	5. c	6. b	7. c	8. b	9. b	10. c
28	1. b	2. a	3. a	4. c	5. c	6. c	7. b	8. c	9. a	10. a
29	1. c	2. b	3. a	4. c	5. c	6. c	7. c	8. c	9. c	10. a
30	1. a	2. a	3. b	4. a	5. a	6. b	7. c	8. a	9. a	10. a
31	1. c	2. a	3. a	4. b	5. a	6. a	7. b	8. a	9. a	10. c
32	1. a	2. b	3. b	4. a	5. a	6. b	7. b	8. a	9. b	10. c
33	1. c	2. b	3. b	4. c	5. b	6. b	7. a	8. c	9. a	10. b
34	1. c	2. a	3. c	4. b	5. c	6. c	7. a	8. a	9. c	10. c
35	1. b	2. a	3. c	4. a	5. b	6. c	7. a	8. a	9. c	10. b
36	1. b	2. c	3. a	4. b	5. a	6. c	7. a	8. b	9. c	10. b
37	1. c	2. b	3. c	4. b	5. a	6. a	7. b	8. c	9. a	10. a
38	1. b	2. c	3. b	4. b	5. b	6. a	7. a	8. a	9. c	10. b
39	1. c	2. c	3. c	4. a	5. b	6. c	7. c	8. c	9. c	10. b
40	1. a	2. c	3. a	4. a	5. b	6. a	7. b	8. a	9. c	10. c
41	1. b	2. a	3. a	4. a	5. c	6. b	7. b	8. b	9. a	10. a
42	1. b	2. a	3. a	4. c	5. c	6. a	7. b	8. c	9. a	10. c
43	1. b	2. a	3. c	4. b	5. c	6. a	7. c	8. b	9. b	10. c
44	1. c	2. a	3. c	4. b	5. c	6. b	7. a	8. b	9. c	10. a
45	1. c	2. a	3. c	4. a	5. b	6. b	7. c	8. a	9. b	10. a
46	1. b	2. c	3. c	4. b	5. c	6. c	7. c	8. c	9. a	10. c
47	1. b	2. a	3. c	4. c	5. b	6. a	7. b	8. a	9. a	10. b
48	1. c	2. b	3. b	4. c	5. c	6. b	7. a	8. a	9. b	10. a
49	1. c	2. a	3. a	4. b	5. b	6. b	7. c	8. c	9. c	10. b
50	1. b	2. a	3. b	4. c	5. a	6. c	7. b	8. c	9. a	10. a

Progress Graph (1–25)

Directions: Write your comprehension score in the box under the selection number. Then put an x on the line above each box to show your reading time and words-per-minute reading rate.

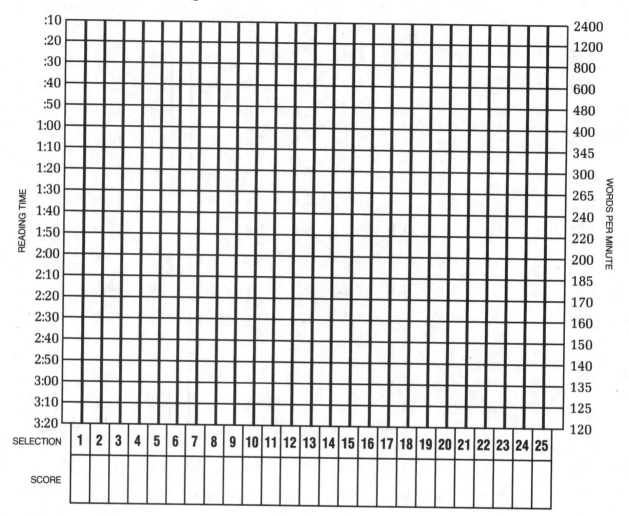

:10																								2400
:20																								1200
:30																								800
:40																								600
:50																								480
1:00																								400
1:10																								345
1:20																								300
1:30																								265
1:40																								240
1:50																								220
2:00																								200
2:10																								185
2:20																								170
2:30																								160
2:40																								150
2:50																								140
3:00																								135
3:10																								125
3:20																								120

READING TIME

WORDS PER MINUTE

SELECTION | 1 | 2 | 3 | 4 | 5 | 6 | 7 | 8 | 9 | 10 | 11 | 12 | 13 | 14 | 15 | 16 | 17 | 18 | 19 | 20 | 21 | 22 | 23 | 24 | 25

SCORE

118

Progress Graph (26–50)

Directions: Write your comprehension score in the box under the selection number. Then put an x on the line above each box to show your reading time and words-per-minute reading rate.

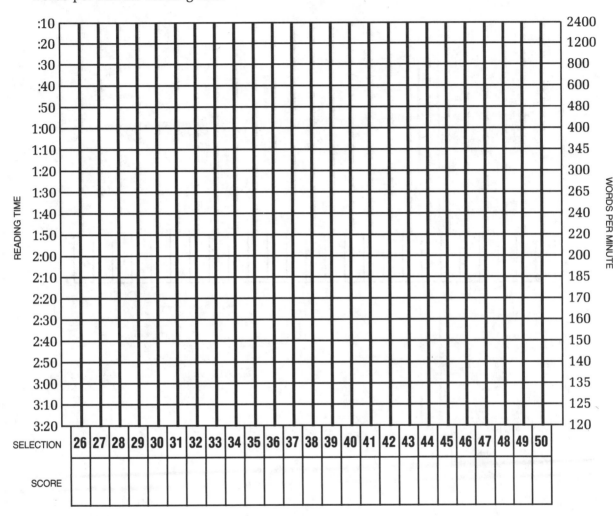

READING TIME		WORDS PER MINUTE
:10		2400
:20		1200
:30		800
:40		600
:50		480
1:00		400
1:10		345
1:20		300
1:30		265
1:40		240
1:50		220
2:00		200
2:10		185
2:20		170
2:30		160
2:40		150
2:50		140
3:00		135
3:10		125
3:20		120

SELECTION: 26 27 28 29 30 31 32 33 34 35 36 37 38 39 40 41 42 43 44 45 46 47 48 49 50

SCORE

Pacing Graph

Directions: In the boxes labeled "Pace" along the bottom of the graph, write your words-per-minute rate. On the vertical line above each box, put an x to indicate your comprehension score.

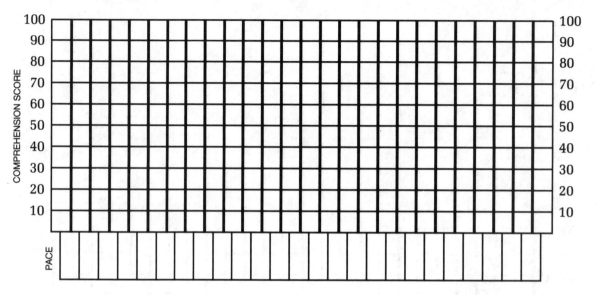